COUNSELING IN GENDERLAND

A Guide for You and Your Transgendered Client

$29.95

This book is dedicated to my daughter, Jenny Horn (1963-1984), who taught me about grace under pressure, about living with difference, and about the indomitability of the human spirit.

ACKNOWLEDGMENTS

There are so many persons who had both a direct and an indirect influence on the production of this book. I would like to thank them all and apologize in advance if I have inadvertently omitted anyone who feels s/he belongs here.

THANKS TO:

My clients who are my constant teachers and an extraordinary group of human beings.

My mentors and teachers in the field of humanistic psychology

Jenny Stevens and Anne Woolf, who literally pulled this book out of me, helped shape it and publish it and without whom this project would never have left the ground.

The courageous leaders of the gender community with whom I have worked, laughed, argued, and shared hugs, especially Ariadne Kane, Alison Laing, Betty Ann Lind, Merissa Sherrill Lynn, and Virginia Prince.

Mariette Pathy Allen, photographer extraordinaire, friend and fellow traveler in this interesting world in which she has helped so many individuals discover their beauty.

Richard Docter, who has been "going where no man has gone before" in his pioneering research and writings, and has a heart as big as California, where he resides and works when he is not appearing voluntarily at various gender conferences and events.

Sheila Kirk, MD, who is creating a dialogue between the medical community and those in the gender community who need its services and who is doing pioneering research in many areas of gender identity.

Roger Millen, colleague and friend, whose knowledge of body energy and psycholinguistics brought new insight and contributions to me and to this community.

David Seil, MD, a compassionate colleague and helpful critic.

Janis Walworth, a fellow traveler in this world.

Elke O'Donnell, who helped me integrate Jungian process-oriented psychology into our work with the transgendered.

And to my many polygender friends who combine the strength of the warrior, the softness of their vulnerability and nurturance, and the creativity of the artist.

PREFACE

Background

People often ask me how I happened to wind up working with individuals exploring their gender identity.

I realize I have answered this question in many different ways, all of which are true but none of which I have said all at one time! So, here, for the record, are my responses.

One day, when I was about twelve, I arrived home from school (Elizabeth Barrett Browning Junior High, known affectionately to us as "Everything But Boys") and found my mother and father playing. He was sitting in the living room adorned with earrings and lipstick.

I was shocked. I burst out crying.

He was amused at my reaction: "It's just a game, a bit of silliness." But, for me, though I could not put it into words at the time, my familiar, masculine, handsome, safe Daddy had suddenly become Other, something for which I had no context. He was utterly amazed at my reaction.

Years later, when I started working with the wives and partners of crossdressers, that experience helped me understand the kind of disorientation that is so common among women whose partners present as Other.

****

I had a daughter, Jenny Horn, who died in 1984 at the age of 21. She had a condition called neurofibromatosis, which produced differences in her body and appearance from the children around her. She was often teased and felt isolated. Not until she was a teenager did she ever meet anyone else with her condition. When she finally developed the sarcoma that sometimes accompanies the original disorder (and eventually killed her), she was, again, alone.

At that time we knew no one else in the NF community who had NF sarcoma. This experience gave me an exquisite sensitivity to persons with differences. Because I was so close to her, I did not relate to her through her condition, but as an interesting young human being whom I loved.

Later I was able to understand the difficulties of persons with gender differences and those of their significant others who must also struggle out of fear and isolation to find their own communities within a basically hostile society.

****

I became a Gestalt therapist in 1970: I worked at the Associates for Human Resources, Inc., in Concord, MA, for twelve years as a therapist, organization development consultant, trainer, workshop designer, facilitator, and instructor in a graduate degree program.

Just before I left AHR in 1981, having made the decision to be an independent counselor and consultant, I met Ariadne Kane, director of the Outreach Institute of Gender Studies, through a mutual friend at an AHP (Association for Humanistic Psychology) conference. Suddenly the door to a whole new fascinating world was opened.

Ari and I started working together to bring humanistic psychology into the gender field, and vice versa. We made presentations at AHP conferences. He came to AHR to work with a long time ongoing group of mine where he appeared both as a conventional appearing male and crossdressed. Then in 1982 he invited me to attend an event in Provincetown, Mass., called Fantasia Fair, which he had created eight years previously. He asked me to meet with the wives and partners of the crossdressers at this event. At that time, nobody was paying much attention to these women. Indeed, when we did get together, the women there had never talked to anyone else about their husbands, and a lot of crying and disclosure went on.

For six of the fourteen years I have been working at the Fair, I met with these wonderful women who formed a close bond and have supported each other over time. After that, they were ready to run their own group and help women who were new to the Fair.

That first year, I spoke with many crossdressers, and absorbed a lot of information. I witnessed deep feelings, theirs and my own, about what it means to be a person with gender difference in this society.

On the last night of my stay in Provincetown, after everyone had gone home, I had this dream:

In front of the inn where I am staying there is a large rosehip bush (true). I discover a miniature camera hidden inside one of the rosehips. Somehow I am guided to take the film to a camera shop to get it developed. No one is supposed to see me. I look furtively behind me to make sure no one is following me.

When I get the photos back they show a group picture of a secret society of men. A voice tells me that I am never to reveal their identity but am to carry their message to the world.

I knew then that I had something important to do regarding this population, but I never imagined that it would become as central to both my work life and social life as it did.

A short while after I had this dream, I spoke to my former analyst, and he said, "Yes, but what is there about _you_ that has been hidden and needs to be out?" We talked and I realized that I had a secret sexual fantasy of myself performing as a male from time to time. It felt shameful, not normal. Subsequently I discovered that many women play with this fantasy. Eventually I made the discovery that one thing that was unconsciously attracting me to crossdressers was that they could appear as women in women's clothes, but underneath, their maleness lay hidden like a sleeping animal ready to be aroused at any moment.

They were my mirror.

****

My Crossdressing Experience

I became "Neil" for a night at the Fantasy Ball, an event that is held once a year at Fantasia Fair in the fall. It's the time for everyone to dress up as alternate personae, and a wide range of characters shows up. It is open to the public. This was just my second fair.

What was so surprising was that, though I had spent almost a week with these folks, no one recognized me. What had I done? I had donned a shirt and tie, worn my own pants and sports jacket, and put on a false moustache. My hair was short and unisex. I wore no makeup. I was surprised that a few little changes would produce such a complete disguise.

Later, I took off my outer garments and became an androgynous figure. (I had a latex tank suit on underneath. I am well endowed so the juxtaposition of moustache and breasts was startling, I'm sure.)

A young woman approached me and told me that her mother, who was sitting at the bar, was quite upset. She had wondered why "us guys" would want to create such prominent breasts. It seemed like a mockery of women to her. I laughed and told the young woman to tell her mom it was the breasts that were real; the rest was the disguise! I watched as the mom's mouth fell open and she blushed bright red.

What is there about mixed gender attributes and expression that absolutely throws us for a loop? We live in a society that is so trained to respond to the visual that we can hardly see beyond it to the real person!

Orientation

My training and value system is linked up with the field of humanistic psychology* with which I have been involved since 1967.

Humanistic psychology focuses on the potential of the individual. It addresses the possibilities of the future more than the pathology or dysfunctions of the past. It also increasingly recognizes the importance of social change and the interdependence of all living beings.

When a transgender client comes to a humanistic practitioner, the model for the counseling work is educational. The client is a student and the counselor is a consultant/educator. The curriculum is the self of the client. The counselor has skills, resources and experience to offer. The client brings ideas about what he needs to learn or discover. The counselor respects and supports the client's ability to take responsibility for himself.

Another useful metaphor is seeing the client and counselor like partners in a detective agency. They have a number of clues and are trying to figure out what the situation actually is. They often have to find out about the background of those they are investigating (in this case, the client and the client's family) in order to understand the present circumstances.

*See Appendix for more information about humanistic psychology

The counseling relationship in humanistic psychology is an interactive one in which both parties bring their whole selves to the interaction. The client's strengths and potential are an important aspect of the process. The counselor uses her own images, feelings, and genuine responses to enhance the dialogue. Discoveries get made on both sides.

When someone goes to a psychiatrist or psychoanalyst, the predominant model is medical. The client is a patient and the professional is a doctor who is supposedly there to help bring about a cure, who sometimes prescribes drugs, and whose job it is to diagnose, analyze and decide a course of treatment.

Just as gayness is not a disease to be cured (as it once was viewed by psychoanalysis) so gender difference, I believe, is another aspect of diversity which is slowly becoming recognized as legitimate and possibly prenatally determined. Gays and transgendered folks can have many emotional problems from living in a hostile society and from having to deal with loss of loved ones. But this suggests a need for social change and emotional support, not a need to revise the identity of the client or deal with his/her difference as though it were an illness.

Nevertheless, gender identity issues and expression are still treated somewhat as disorders or illnesses in the DSM IV. That is slowly being changed. Make sure to familiarize yourself with the current diagnostic categories. You will need to decide how to make use of that information, if at all, for insurance companies.*

*For various psychoanalytic theories of transvestism and transsexualism see Richard Docter's book, *Transvestites and Transsexuals* noted in bibliography.

For transgendered individuals, the humanistic learning model seems to work very well in bringing issues to the foreground and enabling clients to take primary responsibility for working out their path. They do not want their gender identity search to be viewed as an illness but more as a personal and spiritual growth voyage for which they need a caring, sensitive, knowledgeable helpmate and guide--you.

The Language Predicament

"But 'glory' doesn't mean a nice, knockdown argument" Alice objected.

"When I use a word," Humpty Dumpty said, in a rather scornful tone, "it means just what I choose it to mean--neither more nor less."

"The question is" said Alice "whether you can make words mean so many different things."

"The question is" said Humpty Dumpty "which is to be master-- that's all."

From the writings of
Lewis Carroll

In the minds of many persons, confusion exists regarding the difference between sex and gender. The words are often used interchangeably. However, one's sex is biologically determined (and even here, there can be confusion with intersexed persons who have the biological characteristics of both sexes, and persons who have irregular chromosome patterns!) and designated, in most cases, as male or female. Gender is a highly subjective perception of oneself as a man or a woman. It involves internal feelings, external role behavior and, most important, core identity.

When *gender dysphoria* exists, one experiences an incompatibility between one's anatomical, biological sex and the subjective experience of being masculine or feminine, one's gender identity and role.

It is not within the scope of this book to go into detail about all the variations of sex and gender which exist. (See Richard Docter's book for more background.) In brief, a *primary transsexual* has had a lifelong experience of gender dysphoria, an unhappiness with anatomical sex often accompanied by feelings of intense envy of the opposite sex. This can occur in both males and females who can be either heterosexual or homosexual. (Another myth is that one's gender defines one's *sexual orientation* i.e. all transsexuals and crossdressers must be gay. Gender orientation and sexual orientation are separate and distinct phenomena.)

The *secondary transsexual's* desire for transition arrives later in life. Childhood is free from gender dysphoria. In some cases, a history of fetishistic crossdressing is present. In others, some homosexual eroticism and full time living in the preferred gender role finally leads to a need for a more complete change.

However, secondary transsexuals, unlike primaries, have often achieved satisfaction, for periods of time, in their original gender roles. The move toward transition may often be fueled by stress anxiety and unrealistic idealization of women.

Crossdressers are those who wear articles of the opposite gender.
Transvestites are fetishistic *crossdressers*.
Transgenderists are persons who choose to live in the other gender role.

In this book, I have had the challenge of using pronouns and terms for gender shifting and assignation that have been set by our bi-polar thinking in English i.e. "he" is one thing and "she" is another. The word *transsexual*, which would literally mean crossing from one static biological state to another, is therefore not accurate in describing the phenomenon of gender shifting to which we refer. Kate Bornstein, author, playwright and actor, says it well in the title of one of her theater pieces: *The Opposite Sex is Neither.* However, transsexual is the word that is commonly used to describe what we have defined above. Without inventing an elaborate system of linguistics, I am going to have to use what is available, I'm afraid.

So, I will use *HE* to refer to a male crossdresser regardless of gender choice at the moment. I will use *SHE* to refer to primary transsexuals who have always identified as women. I will use either pronoun arbitrarily when sex or gender is not apparent or is not already designated (e.g. when I refer to counselors).

Although there are female crossdressers and transsexuals, my practice has consisted mainly of males, so these are the persons to whom I will be referring in my discussion.

Femme is the currently recognized word for describing that aspect of a man which needs to express itself as woman.

SRS refers to sex reassignment surgery.

The generic *"T"* will be used when I am speaking about anyone in a gender exploring mode (transvestites, transsexuals, crossdressers, transgenderists).

The word *polygendered*, which I have coined, refers to persons who experience many shifts of gender perception in their lifetime.

I will use *counseling* consistently to refer to what is happening between the helping professional and the client.

Definitions of counseling include:

1. The act of exchanging opinions and ideas; consultation.
2. Advice or guidance, especially as solicited from a knowledgeable person.
3. A plan of action.*

Often *psychotherapy* (the treatment of mental and emotional disorders through the use of psychological techniques designed to encourage communication of conflicts and insight into problems,

*Definitions are from *Websters Unabridged Dictionary*.

xvi

with the goal being personality growth and behavior modification) is a major aspect of the process.

In the Personal Histories section (Part IV) therapy is the word often used by clients. I have not changed or edited their language.

So for now, Humpty Dumpty, I join you in asserting my role as the master of these words in this book---but I don't like it and hope, some day, that a gender linguist takes on the vast assignment of restructuring our language to reflect the reality of sex and gender diversity.

FOREWORD

Once upon a time, a very capable gender counselor sat down to write a book to help her colleagues. This is the book she wrote, and it incorporates not only her own insights, but much information about crossdressers, transsexuals, and their loved ones.

If you are going to travel into Genderland, you will be well advised to take this map along. It provides suggested starting points, alternative routes of travel, and practical recommendations on how to proceed.

There is something a little different about experiences in Genderland. And so it is important to start with some awareness of how you feel about the journey. After all, most of us have grown up in a land that looks upon crossdressers and transsexuals as psychiatric casualties. But if we are to be effective in our counseling efforts, it is important that we examine our own baggage. This book will assist you in making such an appraisal, and it will assist you to see that most crossdressers and transsexuals are struggling with the same kinds of growth issues as touch the lives of all of us.

There is plenty of evidence that counselors of all professional orientations may benefit from a new map of Genderland. For example, while about 50% of the crossdressers responding to a large national survey said they had sought some kind of counseling, most also noted that the helping professionals they saw seemed poorly informed about gender issues. Perhaps our counselor training programs have included too little about gender matters in their curricula.

As a careful and thorough mapmaker, Niela Miller gives us valuable insights into her approaches in working with cross-dressers and transsexuals. From the initial telephone contact through the process of contracting with clients or couples, we are guided through a helping process that is often heavily laden with guilt, shame, uncertain gender identity, and maladaptive struggles to meet competing demands. The goal: To assist the client to integrate a lifestyle and an identity that can encompass not only intense gender motives, but the many other needs that are part of a growing and changing personal development across the life span.

Genderland is a kind of Wonderland with characters and characteristics all its own. Venture forth. Like the journey of life, this trip may offer you experiences and relationships you never expected to have. And while you may have an impact upon your fellow travelers, surely the journey will also have an impact upon you.

Richard F. Docter, Ph.D
Professor of Psychology
California State University, Northridge

TABLE OF CONTENTS

COUNSELING IN GENDERLAND:
A Guide for You and Your Transgendered Client

PART I ENGAGING WITH THE GENDER-EXPLORING CLIENT

PART II- THE COUNSELOR'S PROCESS:
Know Thyself, Know Thy Client

PART I

ENGAGING WITH THE GENDER-EXPLORING CLIENT

"UGH, SERPENT!" (says the Pigeon to Alice)

"But I'm not a serpent, I tell you!" said Alice, "I'm a --- a---"

"Well. What are you?" said the Pigeon. "I can see you're trying to invent something!"

"I --- I'm a little girl," said Alice, rather doubtfully, as she remembered the number of changes she had gone through that day.

"A likely story, indeed!" said the Pigeon, in a tone of the deepest contempt. "I've seen a good many little girls in my time, but never one with such a neck as that! No, no! you're a serpent; and there's no use denying it ..."

From the writings of
Lewis Carroll

INTRODUCTION

My purpose in writing this book is to enable you as counselors to appreciate and understand the unique client with gender identity issues, and the potentially profound effect of these issues on you as a person and helping professional. Inasmuch as you are able to address all personal and professional issues that are raised for you in response to the persons and material presented, you can be very effective in helping your clients work through a complex life situation of high challenge, diversity, and fascination, and, often, pain.

This book is *not* intended to be an academic treatise about transgenderism. Therefore, technical information will be at a minimum. (I refer you to the excellent resources, including a bibliography, listed in the back of the book.)

However, it is useful to have some sense of the great range of gender experience and expression that you, as a counselor, may come across in your practice.

My own counseling experience has been primarily with male crossdressers and transsexual women (i.e., born biologically male, identifying as women) so I will be using material that specifically references these groups.

Within these groups, variations of expression take place. For instance, there are male crossdressers who are interested in only one or two items of clothing to the exclusion of all others. They may wear pantyhose every day to work under their trousers, and this gives them the relief they need. Or they may come home and slip into a nightgown, watch TV, and not feel the need for anything more extensive. Some will fully dress but not use wigs or makeup. Others must do everything completely or they are not satisfied. Still others will use only makeup and jewelry but not change clothes. One client wore women's clothes below the waist, and his regular men's clothes (also a moustache) above. Many will have erotic feelings associated with dressing. Some will simply feel more relaxed and comfortable.

Most crossdressers with a strong masculine identity are not interested in changing their bodies. Some who are transsexually inclined might want to have electrolysis, and some of this group might want to take hormones for breast development. They usually have no interest in changing their genitals (unless, along the way, they realize that they are transsexual after all, which can happen when a man finds more satisfaction in his femme role than he does in his manhood, and discovers how painful it is for him to return to his usual role in society and in his family). If this dysphoria becomes exceedingly strong, he may opt for a radical change. Counseling is imperative for this type of individual.

Among the uninformed, one of the strongest misconceptions about crossdressers is that they are gay. Most are heterosexual just like the population at large. It is important to separate sexual orientation (body response to others) from gender orientation (in the brain/mind). Although crossdressing can certainly affect a man's sexual fantasies, i.e., imagining himself in woman's role being made love to, his empathy and attraction toward women often produce long and devoted partnerships.

For transsexuals, an equal amount of variation of expression exists as it does among crossdressing males. Some are utterly

4

uninterested in clothes, others are passionate about them. Sounds like the range in nontransgendered women, doesn't it? What is important to these folks is body image, i.e., getting rid of male characteristics such as body hair (especially on the face), acquiring breasts, and, for some, acquiring a constructed vagina.

Although I will not be discussing female to male transitions in this book, I do want to mention that more and more biological females who consider themselves men are coming out now, having finally resolved that they are not butch lesbians but are actually men. Some have secondary sex characteristics of men; many do not, but feel like men anyway. They transition by having mastectomies and taking hormones to produce facial hair, the opposite of male to female transsexuals. The genital surgery for females to males has still not progressed as far as that of male-to-female, but there are several choices for them, and some have decided to go ahead with surgery.

In order to clear up confusion that exists in the mainstream, and also among practitioners, it is important to mention drag queens. These are men, usually gay, who dress as women to be entertainers, called female impersonators. Many of the movies that have been made about gender expression feature drag queens (*Priscilla, Queen of the Desert* and *To Wong Foo...* are recent examples).

But drag queens do not have the same psyches as crossdressers. When they are not on stage, their interest in dressing is usually not present. Crossdressers, on the other hand, have a deep desire to express a femme aspect of their being through dressing. It can appear at any time in their life. It is often a private act, very different from the drag queen (for whom it is always a public act.) Many drag queens don't perform but dress

5

for parties, a night out, or even wear women's robes, etc. in their own homes.

The last group, transgenderists, are basically those who live full time in the role of the other gender but who may or may not make body changes. One person I know well lives half time as a woman, the other half as a man.

Many persons in the gender community use great ingenuity to satisfy the femme who needs to express herself. As a good counselor, you can be supportive of how much imagination and creativity it takes for your gender clients to find a lifestyle that works well for them.

You may even find, as I have, that your own responses to life's vicissitudes become more varied and creative as a result of working with your clients!

This book is highly subjective and one person's experience and approach to what is still a relatively new field of counseling. As such, there are many unanswered questions, unproved theories, and differences of emphasis. I have highlighted aspects of the work which are of particular interest to me and said very little about other areas about which I hope you will read in the excellent bibliography in the appendix.

As you go through the book, jot down your own feelings, questions, reactions. These are of great value in your work with yourself and supervisors, and will hopefully lead to more research and experimentation.

In the following pages, you will find some practical information which is not meant to be a prescription for your behavior, but simply a start at comparing what you might encounter with this particular client group to those with whom you have typically worked, and to share some of my experience and tools I have found useful as food for thought.

We will start at the beginning of the counselor relationship with first contacts and contracting.

CHAPTER 1

BEGINNINGS

Phone Styles

Unless you meet a potential client at a social event, the telephone is usually the first contact. Here are the "styles" I have encountered:

Me: Hello. This is Niela Miller.

    (1)   Silence. Hang up.

    (2)   Hello, I got your name from *Transgender Tapestry*.* Can you tell me what you do?

    (3)   Hello, I'm a crossdresser and my wife hates what I do, but I've been doing it since I was a kid and... (on and on)

    (4)   Hello, could you tell me how much you charge for counseling?

    (5)   Can you tell me how I can get hormones (or SRS)?

    The voices can vary from shaky and barely audible to defiant and challenging, though that is the exception. You

*A major publication for this population. See Appendix.

can pretty much assume that making this call is one of the hardest things this individual has ever done.

Here are some general guidelines for responding.

- Thanks for calling. I will try to give you the information you need to decide whether you want to come see me or not.

- You are not alone. There are many other persons with stories very much like yours.

- Specifically, what do you need to ask me to determine whether you want to set up an appointment?

Two examples follow of what might be covered in that first phone call. This will vary a lot depending on the state of the caller and on your style. Just bear in mind that the person may not be thinking very clearly because he is scared to death. So it does help to be specific, concrete, and even to encourage the person to repeat what he has heard.

I answer the telephone, and the caller says, "Uhh-Uh-hello. I saw your name in *Transgender Tapestry*." Then there's a long pause.

I say, "How can I help you?"

Caller, "Well, what is it you do, exactly?"

I might say, "Let me start with what I don't do. I don't help people put their outfits or makeup together. I don't take them to stores or on other errands that have to do with their gender

10

expression. There are consultants who can help you with these concerns. I'm a counselor and I counsel people about gender issues and life adjustment issues. What would you like to know about that?"

Caller: "Well, uh, what does it cost?"

I tell the person my usual hourly fee, and then I say, "Is that going to be a problem for you?" Then the caller may say "No," or possibly, "Oh, I can't afford that." At this point I provide the caller with options.

I might say, "Well, I have several options for you. One is that I do have a sliding scale if you have limited resources. But if you use the sliding scale, I need you to be very committed to the process because I have limited time. The other thing I can do is to refer you to another colleague of mine who may be able to see you for a lower fee. How do you feel about that?"

Suppose he now says, "I've heard a lot about you and you are really the person who I want to see."

I generally suggest that the person come in for one session so we can see how we "click," whether we can work well with each other. At that time I'll answer any questions he has and tell him something about the way I work. Two out of three do not follow through at the time. Sometimes they will be ready later.

A different kind of call is from someone who says, "I'm a transsexual. I am going for surgery, but I need to see somebody for a certain amount of time in order to be approved*, so I am calling you."

*See Benjamin *Standards of Care* in Appendix

To this person I say, "I appreciate your situation. However, you need to understand that I'm interested in working only with people who really want to work on themselves. All of us have work to do on ourselves, whether it's a requirement or not, particularly people who are going through such a large change in their lives. I'm certainly willing to do one session with you without any obligation for you to commit yourself beyond that. However, if all you want to do is put in time so you can get a letter, I'm really not the right person for you. I can give you the names of some other people who might be willing to meet your requirements, but I strongly advise you against this course of action." In this way I explain the basis on which I am willing to take clients, and I can check their responses.

The First Session--Completing the Contract

When the person actually comes in for the first session, after establishing a friendly and supportive atmosphere, I explain what his/her responsibility is, what I do, and the different ways I work. I may ask some questions about any prior experience with counseling. I also ask how often the person can afford to come during the month. Some people come once a month, some every two weeks; some need to come once a week. If they like that flexibility, then this is a good match. If it drives them crazy, then it's not. If they come from a distance, I am willing to see them for two hours less frequently, which will make their traveling worth it. Time and money issues are worked out during the first session. Make your requirements and theirs clear right at the beginning.

Gathering Information

During the first part of our work together, I might ask my client some or all of the following questions:

- Describe your first crossdressing experience (or transsexual feeling).

- Make a diagram of your family, starting with grandparents and any outstanding information about mental or physical disability, addictions, sex or gender differences, character eccentricities. (I will often make the diagram as the client feeds me information.)

- Describe how you see yourself in your dreams (male, female, both).

- What are your major discomforts in your life?

- What are your greatest strengths as a man? en femme?

- What are your fears and limitations (in each aspect)?

- What does each part think of the other?

- What is your vision of your future?

- How do you feel you have grown/changed in the past year?

- Who are the persons to whom you are closest? How many of them know about your gender difference? What are your beliefs about having them know/not know?

- What kind of friendship or support would you like to give or get from other TV/TS's?

- In what ways do you feel you need to work on yourself to feel the best you can about you?

- How do you deal with your "negative" feelings (shame, guilt, resentment, hostility, anger, jealousy, grief, fear)?

- How do you react to persons of a different color, religion, or sexual orientation, those who are disabled or deformed, with different values?

- If you are married or in a relationship, how open and communicative are you with your partner about your needs, feelings, thoughts? How encouraging are you with your partner to express herself? Are you able to listen without arguing?

- How willing are you to help others like yourself through sharing your experiences, counseling, contributing time and money to gender organizations?

You can use your discretion with the particular client as to when to collect this information and which questions to ask.

Involving the Partner

In counseling a "T" who is in a significant relationship, it is very important for you to see that other person as well.

If there is resistance on the part of the partner, you might instruct the "T" to go home and say to his wife, "My counselor feels that you would be very helpful in giving her information about me that I don't feel I can provide on my own. Would you be willing to help me in that way? This is not about doing counseling with you; it's for you to help us be able to look at my issues and to speak for yourself."

If a woman has feelings for this person, she will probably not refuse. In fact, she will actually feel positive about coming.

Getting her to come to counseling becomes more difficult when she is the one who has driven him to seek therapy. She may refuse to come, saying that he is the one with the problem, let him get cured! Then he might need to respond to her, "My counselor does not feel that she can do good work with me unless she meets you, because you are the other half of the equation. Even if you come only once, it's important for her to know you and for you to speak for yourself, and important for me too."

Very few of my clients' "significant others" has ever refused these two approaches.

If the wife absolutely refuses, I tell the "T" that there are some risks involved if I see him without the partner. The major risk is that they will grow further and further apart as he understands his feelings and his needs and begins to assert them in some way. Unless his wife is part of that process and is able to respond and work issues out with him, it's not very likely that they will be able to continue together.

He may also need to risk trying new activities, such as joining some clubs and meeting other people like himself. If she doesn't understand what those resources are and why they are important to him (and hear it from someone other than him), additional conflict is likely to develop.

The Couples Contract

Another issue in dealing with couples is how you contract with the clients. If you are going to see them together *and* apart, it must be understood that anything that impacts their relationship with each other needs to be spoken about freely in their joint session.

In other words, I do not want to be a secret-keeper for either one of them. Even though I am not going to repeat every single thing that's talked about in the individual sessions, any important material that has to do with their communication, their life style, or their progress on the gender issue that either one of them explores in their individual session must be brought into the joint session.

If they can't agree to that, I can't work with them. It is very important that each partner agrees that nothing is being withheld that is going to affect their decision-making and their feelings about being in the relationship.

If either person breaks this agreement by confiding in you in the absence of the other partner, they can be encouraged by you to tell the partner in your presence or by themselves. If they refuse, they cannot continue to work with you. The left-out partner can be encouraged to seek the truth about the partner's reason for leaving. It is a risk for everyone to enter into this type of arrangement, especially if both clients come. On the other hand, in this particular type of work with gender issues, the advantages of seeing each and both outweigh the risks. Most of the time it works out. (More about this in Part III.)

Commitment

The issue of commitment shows up right at the first contact. Often the clients have a lot of ambivalent feelings. Even once they are at the office, there are several ways you can see that they are having a problem with commitment:

- The conversation remains very general.
- It goes around in circles.
- Whenever there's a possibility of reaching greater depth in exploring an issue, the client retreats.
- The tone of voice is slow and hesitant, or fast without pause.
- The client seems very passive.
- The subject keeps changing.
- The client turns to the counselor for answers.
- The counselor begins to feel bored.

Here are some examples of statements that the counselor can make when she/he suspects that there is a commitment problem:

- It feels like we are going around in circles. Does talking about this really matter to you?
- It doesn't seem like you have much interest in exploring this today. Is that true?
- What would you really like to be doing or talking about now?

A client can be having resistant, confused feelings and still be committed to the counseling process. You know you have a committed client when she arrives on time, brings up what is on her mind without a lot of prompting from you, indicates that she has thought about or acted upon the material from prior sessions, and is reliable about paying for the sessions. I often suggest that clients keep a journal which helps them record their thoughts, feelings, dreams, and progress over time. Doing this is also is an indication of commitment.

Setting Goals

After contracting with a gender exploring client, the next step is setting goals.

Some clients have very poorly formulated goals. They are not even sure why they're there, except that they <u>have</u> to be there.

Others can't discuss their goals, but can just say they have certain feelings with which they are not comfortable.

You can help them determine what their goals are from what they express about their feelings. I point out that this is an ongoing process, and we may change or add goals, but we need to begin with some goals. For instance, one goal might be for the client to learn how to use the counseling process well, so there will be some new learning involved.

One client expressed the feeling that crossdressing interfered too much with his life style. He has a very high level position and travels a lot. When he dresses, it takes a lot of time and preparation; he can't just pack clothes and accessories, then throw them on and throw them off; the psychological transitions are too traumatic.

His goal became trying to find another way, which wasn't so stressful, to honor his femme aspect.

In other words, instead of externalizing a feminine image through clothes and makeup, he imagines an inner woman, a representative of his feminine soul. He might have dialogues with her or feel her presence as a living part of himself. He develops a relationship through dialogue with this archetypal figure who is there any time he cares to turn his attention to her. She can be thought of as a goddess, a queen, a priestess or simply the feminine twin of himself.

Occasionally I have a crossdressing client who says, "I want to be cured. I've had it. I can't stand this any more. Just help me get rid of this problem." (Expressing the desire to be cured is a way for the client to tell me that s/he is unable to manage the transgendered behavior.)

I have to answer that, in my experience, crossdressing behavior is not a disease; it is an aspect of the person's formed identity and is not likely to disappear.

It does have to be managed. However, a more realistic goal might be learning to be comfortable with this aspect of himself which, after all, has always been there. It's unrealistic to assume that transgendered behavior such as crossdressing is simply going to disappear, especially by magic thinking or a few words from me. The old joke--"Make me a malted." "Poof, you're a malted"-- doesn't work.

It helps to find out precisely what the crossdresser is doing now to express his femme side, what feels out of control, what he would like to be able to do and the choices he has for making his life work.

Here is a sampling of goals which have been formulated by my crossdressing clients with my help.

- Accepting himself as he is and being aware of how that is.

- Becoming a member of the crossgender community; coming out of isolation.

- If he has a partner, bringing her in to the process, while also attending to the counseling partnership, conscious and unconscious.

- Understanding his original family's lessons about dealing with stress, secrecy, pain, feelings in general, intimacy and what he has inherited.

- Being conscious of what is and isn't working, his past and present behavior and his future goals. Making choices and creating experiments to enable his life to work <u>now</u>, not someday when he is "she" or may live as a woman.

- Feeling connected to his body, mind, emotions and spirit.

With a transsexual, the challenge is to help the person form a clear identity and to help her determine whether she wants to transition (i.e. go through any of the steps of physical and social role change such as electrolysis, hormone therapy, living as a woman and sex reassignment surgery.) There are a lot of factors governing this decision, but one thing is for sure: living with this condition makes it highly likely that your client will experience constant distress and will need to find a way to resolve this dilemma so that life is not just bearable, but offers some rewards. Many transsexuals feel suicidal at the point at which they seek counseling; their desperation has driven them to your door. With your help, they can sort out what they really want and need and can begin to take steps to bring about these desired circumstances.

Clarifying Who Is Responsible

Many persons from the gender community who come into counseling have no idea of what the counseling process is about.

They assume they are going to initiate the process, and the counselor is going to guide their lives and tell them what they are, what they should do.

They need to learn that, basically, *they're* responsible for the process, not the counselor.

Some people have trouble with the counseling process; others take to it right away.

Your responsibility , among others, is to teach them *how to learn* in this situation, not tell them what they are about (which is what we are going to discover together through the learning process).

Overdependence

If the client has never been involved in any counseling process, then the counselor has to, paradoxically, teach the client how to lead the process.

Depending on whether the client seems to be overly dependent or overly independent, the counselor might respond differently.

For instance, if the client gives evidence of being a very dependent type, the counselor might say, "I notice that you are deferring to me a lot and really depending on me to give you the answers or tell you what to do. I'll help you, but you have to take responsibility for defining and working on your own problem, whatever it is."

If the client asks the counselor to define the problem, the counselor generally responds by asking that client to make a statement for himself.

Sometimes the client depends on the counselor to draw him out. So the counselor might say, "You seem to be relying on me to continually ask you questions."

Recently I had such a client. For the conversation to go on, I said, "Maybe you can think about what you want to talk about, bring up issues, and make a statement. Then I will base my questions on what you say to me."

Overindependence

The opposite kind of client is one who won't let the counselor get a word in edgewise, who talks and talks without a pause. He tries to analyze his whole situation, label himself, and say everything about who and what he is.

So then the feedback is quite different: "I'm noticing you seem to be carrying yourself on your own back. You've come to me because I have a lot of experience; perhaps we could stop periodically and see whether what you are saying is in accordance with my experience as a counselor so I can give you feedback. You don't need to feel so super-responsible that there's no room for feedback from me."

Unless clients learn basic skills and develop confidence in the counseling process, they will not go away from a helping relationship better equipped to help themselves in the future.

Once they have acquired the necessary skills, clients must be weaned away from the counselor so they can feel confident to help themselves.

Saying Goodby

At the onset of counseling, it is important to discuss how we will know when we have completed our work together. The person may then go on to other kinds of help or growth.

Generally saying goodby is appropriate when the person has achieved balance in handling the affairs of his life, including his gender expression. The client feels centered, and the overbearing narcissism that often accompanies this "T" proclivity has been modified in some way so that this person shows signs of caring about other people and about the community.

When I see indications of reaching out to others, not just focusing totally on the self, I know a kind of maturity has taken place.

A person ready to end counseling has eliminated fear, shame, or guilt about "T" behavior. Of course, s/he may have the ordinary human fear about stressful situations; all of us have that. If you hear somebody entering your house late at night, it's natural to be afraid; but a well-balanced person has many more tools and options for handling situations of discomfort and fear, and is not plagued by constant worry or anxiety.

One of the signposts of people who first come for counseling is that very few of them have intimate friends or people with whom they have felt free to talk about their real selves.

So one of the ways of knowing that somebody may be at the end of the counseling process is that they have made good friends. They have told the significant people in their lives. They have no more need to commit sins of omission, or to keep this most important aspect of themselves from the people who really matter to them. They are able to relate to people on a much deeper level.

Previous relationships may have been superficial, utilitarian, or totally controlled. Once the ability to share one's real self is there, the relationships become much more satisfying. They become much deeper; they tend to last a longer time.

The client will demonstrate an ability to bring up feelings and issues he has with you and work them through. In my orientation, Gestalt therapy, these are known as projections. Psychoanalysts would call this transference. As in any other client-counselor relationship, these issues will, of course, come up with your gender clients. One of my colleagues reported a situation in which her crossdressing client felt very critical of the way my colleague dressed and looked (i.e. no make-up, short hair, slacks). This led to a valuable discussion about the range of presentations of "real women" and the stereotypes held by the client which also included a rejection of any type of expression closer to his own masculine self.

Another noticeable factor is that there are no distractions from one part of a person's life to another. The person can be fully present with whatever he or she is doing. So, at work, the "T" isn't constantly thinking about the next time he is going to be dressing. When he is working, his mind is on his work; when he is dressing, he is thoroughly enjoying that and is not preoccupied with other things.

The decision to end counseling is a mutual one. The client may actually say that he feels almost ready to leave. Then, if the counselor has some concerns, she shares them with the client. I may suggest that we do two or three more sessions. If we both agree by the third session that we've pretty much finished what needs finishing, then I'll totally support the client with whatever he needs to do next.

Unfortunately, some clients just disappear. If this happens, it's important that you, the counselor, do not blame yourself. It behooves us to be as aware as possible about what was happening at the time of the disappearance. Sometimes clients lose their jobs and can no longer pay for sessions. Most commonly, the client gets scared of having to take some next step in being responsible for his behavior, and runs away. The gender-exploring client who does simply stop coming may find it very difficult to respond to phone calls or letters from the counselor, but it is important to write an acknowledgement of what has happened and request that the client return for a closing session. In that way you have acted responsibly and done what you can.

CHAPTER 2

UNDERSTANDING THE CLIENT'S AGENDA

Initial Motivation

Many transgendered people have told me that they would not have come to counseling unless they were desperate. They simply came to a dead end. Many, especially transsexuals, start feeling suicidal.

A crossdresser might be in the middle of a marital crisis during which the wife puts her foot down and says, "You'd better go get help." The wife often identifies the "T" as the one with the problem, and what she means by "getting help" is "go get rid of your abnormal behavior."

Sometimes it's the woman who comes for counseling, and the "T" doesn't want to be involved with the process; but the woman wants to know what's going on, how to handle the situation.

Often when potential clients call, they disguise their names, or they make an appointment and then get cold feet and don't show up.

It is the unusual "T" who comes in a positive frame of mind because he wants to learn about himself and his options. It's a joy to the counselor when this happens.

The Presenting Problem

In counseling, the presenting problem is the new client's statement of why he or she needs counseling.

Often the stated problem is either the "tip of the iceberg" or just one part of a much larger syndrome.

For example, sometimes people think they're coming to counseling for a gender problem when they actually have other dysfunctions that need attending to. They procrastinate or they keep losing their jobs or they have no friends, and they blame it all on their gender issues.

I point out to them that there are plenty of people with severe gender dysphoria who are very successful in their work lives and also have active social lives. They need to separate other problems from their gender issues.

Other clients come in who are quite free from shame. For instance, they enjoy crossdressing behavior, but are concerned that it is bringing pain to the people who are close to them.

With crossdressers, the problem usually has to do with relationship issues or with some fear about being caught or recognized. With the transgendered individual, the problem depends on the severity of the dysphoria. It is oppressive for a transsexual to live as a man in society when one actually feels that one is a woman.

Crossdressers typically arrive with one of four major issues:

(1)   They may have discomfort, guilt or shame about the need to crossdress. Often the male side of themselves objects to this kind of behavior; the disapproval is then projected onto everyone else. The result is a male side that is judgmental and contemptuous and a _femme_ side that is full of fantasies and obsessions about crossdressing.

(2)   The crossdresser may have relationship tension with a partner who disapproves and is turned off sexually by crossdressing.

Many crossdressers have sexual fantasies, involving being dressed as a woman while making love, or wearing women's clothes to bed. In fact, many of these men cannot achieve satisfaction without experiencing that fantasy, particularly if they are transsexually inclined.

Sometimes the partner is jealous of the femme persona just as she would be if there were a "mistress."

(3)   A client begins to act impulsively, for instance, by dressing up provocatively and going to a pick-up bar.

Or a transsexually-inclined man
with a family doesn't feel
comfortable about his physical or his
psychological changes, but his need to
express his femininity is very strong.
So he goes on the Internet, pretends he's
a woman, gets "involved" with a man on
line and then has a panic attack because
of a moral imperative to be honest. Such
impulsive behavior may even get this
person into trouble, either with society,
or with his family or partner.

(4)   The "T" may have very poor coping
skills. Crossdressing then becomes the
addiction to take away stress in his life
or to alter his mood, just as would
alcohol.

Is Transition the Answer?*

Many transgendered people who begin therapy arrive at
their wit's end. They feel that life is not worth living if they
cannot solve their problem.

For some transsexuals, it takes quite a time before they
realize that what they are needing is to be in transition, i.e. starting
to move toward womanhood more fully. For others the realization
is immediate. Still others need to work out what they value so
highly in their current lives that they don't want to disturb it in

*It will help you to read some background material. See bibliography of
books on gender identity issues in Appendix.

favor of a complete transition. Some transsexuals will find creative ways to live with the dysphoria, so that they can keep their family intact but at the same time have an adequate way of expressing their womanhood. This might involve taking hormones or getting electrolysis.

Many individuals will choose not to have sex reassignment surgery as long as they keep valuing the other part of their lives where they live essentially as men. Others feel that they have to make radical changes and give up the male part of their lives.

This entire process is a dynamic one. An individual may be at a different point five or ten years later; things may change. I have long since given up predicting what the changes are going to be or trying to steer people in a particular direction. My approach is to stay *closely attuned with the person's process*. The healing factor or the truth about their experience will eventually emerge if there is enough attention paid on the part of both the counselor and the person involved.

Summary of Typical Presenting Problems

• Discomfort, guilt and shame about the need to dress. Conflict between the male side, which is judgmental and contemptuous, and the femme side, which is full of fantasies and obsessions about dressing or changing one's body in various ways.

• Relationship tension with partner who disapproves or is turned off sexually. Sexual fantasies that include being a receptive woman while making love, wearing women's clothes to bed, sometime allowed, often forbidden.

• Jealousy on the part of the spouse, who sees the alternate femme persona as a rival, as more interesting/more desirable to him.

• Denial and dishonesty cause impulsive acting out, which gets the person into trouble either with society or with family.

• Poor coping skills, so that dressing becomes the addiction to take away stress or alter the "T's" mood because he doesn't know how to resolve the life issue or responsibility without high anxiety or stress.

CHAPTER 3

STAGES OF DEVELOPMENT

Certain distinctions can be made between the way the crossdresser develops, and the path of the transsexual. Crossdressers have both an internal predisposition to the behavior coupled with specific objects in the external environment which become invested with meaning and sensation. Transsexualism arises solely as an internal recognition which, if acted upon, then causes the person to adopt certain roles and accessories from the environment. Much of the emotional trauma for the transsexual involves having to adapt her behavior to the gender she is perceived to be by society, i.e. male, in order to function and fit in. There are also distinctions between the primary and secondary transsexual in this regard (see Richard Docter's *Transvestites and Transsexuals* for detailed discussion). The crossdresser, on the other hand, does not have this particular problem but is more plagued by how his chosen femme gender expression affects his relationships.

The Crossdresser

Gender expression takes a variety of forms, and varies from person to person. During the course of my work I have identified typical stages of gender expression in the crossdresser.

1. The person sees something or someone that he wants to make a part of himself, and he reaches for it or has it thrust upon him. He might start by taking a pair of his mother's

panties or nylons, putting them on, and getting a thrill. Or he may have had a sister, or even his mother, dress him up as a little girl. Sometimes, cross-dressing behavior begins when there has been a loss of some kind--the mother has gone to the hospital to have another baby, or the child has been taken to the grandparents for the summer----and it's a way for the child to have some control over keeping the mother close by wearing some of her things.

One researcher of gender identity shifts in young children, Susan Coates, Ph.D.*, found that, in every case that she was investigating, there was either some kind of removal from the mother, or the mother herself went through some kind of trauma within the first few years of the child's life.

Anxiety was created in the child, as was the the need to make sure that he had some kind of control over his mother's nearness. Although he couldn't actually do anything physically about it, he could do something with her clothing. Often the result was a sensual/excited response. In psychoanalytic theory, this substitution of an object for a person is known as fetishism.

2. Stronger feelings arise with dressing than with other activities. I have a theory that

*c/o St. Lukes--Roosevelt Hospital, New York

34

there is something different from other boys about their nervous system and the way they respond to certain clothing items being near their skin. When a child starts this activity, he is not looking in mirrors; it's not visual, it's tactile.

(Suppose men's underwear were made of the same kind of material as women's. Would there still be that distinction of gender expression, or would there be just an attraction to the actual feeling of the garments?)

My intuition says that when other little boys are exposed to this kind of material, it doesn't affect them in the same way. It might relieve some "T"s to know they may have been born with a nervous system that responds to certain kinds of tactile experiences. We need research!

3. The next stage is that the crossdresser forms a repetitive pattern, either in reality or in fantasy. Some people have early experiences, and then their environment does not allow them to manifest the experience. The feeling continues in some way in fantasy, or else it goes underground and then pops up later on.

4. Around pre-puberty and puberty, sexual feelings arise in connection with women's clothes. Sometimes the behavior manifests itself through particular items, usually lingerie or women's shoes, that produce strong sexual feelings or release. This also can be a time when sex and gender identity become confused.

   Young crossdressers may be wondering whether they might be gay (except they're usually not; in fact, attracted to boys). They do wonder what is going on with them. They even feel alone, confused and unable to get information about the way they feel.

5. The next stage might be visual discovery. The person likes to look at himself when he has women's clothing on, and that provides an additional thrill in the experience. A strong sexual component with masturbation almost always accompanies crossdressing starting at puberty. In any case, it is sensual and erotic.

6. In the later levels of development, cross-dressing can become relational and social. Crossdressers start meeting other people like themselves, joining clubs, buying magazines, and recognizing that there are all kinds of "T" activities, social groups, and self-help groups. At this point a peculiar

thing happens: the erotic aspects of crossdressing diminish significantly. That is, the inner feminine nature begins to be addressed.

Of course, some "T"s never come out of the closet. All they want is for their partners in life to accept them as they are, and to be able to dress around the house. If they receive that kind of acceptance (both partners agreeing to keeping it that way), they may not be interested in the social clubs or the group experiences. They simply deal with crossdressing within their lives.

As some people who stay in counseling for awhile learn to handle their stress in a number of ways, their need to crossdress diminishes significantly. But the majority who seek counseling need to come out into their own society; that is, they need to learn that they are not freaks, they are not alone, they are part of a subculture of the larger culture.

As they start learning how to relate to other people, developing good social skills as "T"s, and possibly undoing some of the ways that they used to be in the world as men, they become more congruent with that inner experience.

7. Ultimately, many "T"s arrive at a new
   spiritual level, desiring to serve or help
   others. This type of development is also
   a mark of good health in anyone who goes
   through counseling. That is, at some point,
   after they go through a whole period of self-
   involvement, and work on the self, their
   vision turns outward, and they want to be of
   use to society.

Signs of Integration

One of the questions in counseling "T's" is, "How do you know when someone is well integrated?"

One of the signs, as mentioned above, is that it stops being a self-involved enterprise. The person is now going to take his or her place as a useful member of this society, and maybe even of a larger society. I know one "T" who is interested in communicating with the mainstream, so she writes articles for newspapers and other publications as her contribution.

Some people become political about gender issues. Others will be more interested in the religious questions. Still others will be interested in the sociological questions. Others highlight the issues through artistic expression.

But, in general, a kind of broader-based thinking takes place as questions of spirituality arise: "What is my connection to the whole?" "What is the inner knowledge of the masculine and feminine in me as it is in all human beings?" "What is it that I can contribute to society's understanding about what it means to be fully human?"

In the next few pages you will find a summary of the typical stages of crossdressing behavior and of transsexual development. These are, by no means, exhaustive, but are like road signs, giving you some indication of what to be aware of around the next bend.

Summary of Typical Stages for Crossdressers

1. Childhood: Seeing something/someone which you want to make a part of yourself--reaching for it or having it thrust upon you.

2. Having a sensual, excited or comforted response. Stronger feelings than with other activities.

3. Forming a repetitive pattern (in reality and/or fantasy).

4. Puberty: Discovering sexual feelings in connection with clothes. Fetishistic behavior.

5. Visual imagery: Seeing self, other women through photos, mirrors, in person and having excited, sometimes envious responses, high narcissism.

6. Coming out: Relational and social experience with the "T" culture--loss of mainly erotic feelings associated with dressing.

7. Spiritual and communal: The inner marriage of masculine to feminine, community service, sometimes political activism for human rights, abolition of prejudices about other groups such as gays, blacks, or disabled.

I have focussed on the crossdresser in the previous pages because for the first eight years of my practice they were my main clients. Then transsexuals started to appear. Their evolution is somewhat different.

The Transsexual

1. The young child becomes aware he feels he is of a different gender than his body indicates.

2. The dysphoria increases with all kinds of fantasizing, bargaining with God, wish-making that somehow, magically, things will be put right.

3. Either the child acts out by taking on the social role of the opposite gender and trying everyone's patience and expertise, or the child learns to pretend and lie about its perceived identity as a girl in order to fit in.

4. This latter behavior, the more common, may continue into adulthood, but for some, the dysphoria often becomes unbearable. Suicidal fantasies emerge. At this point, out of desperation, the person will seek counseling, and will make a determination about transitioning.

5. Usually, taking physical steps such as having electrolysis and/or taking hormones brings great relief even if SRS (sex reassignment surgery) is rejected as an alternative because of life circumstances, such as a family. Unfortunately, a certain percentage of transsexuals do become self-destructive or try to by-pass the Benjamin Standards of Care

(see Appendix) in their eagerness to end their torment. Often, their post-surgical adjustment may not be as good as those who received substantial counseling and lived as women prior to making radical changes.

6.   A certain number of transsexuals do decide to go ahead with SRS to feel "complete." Although interested researchers and practitioners are attempting to get a long range view of quality of life issues for this population before and after surgery, there is still not enough information to make definitive statements one way or the other.

CHAPTER 4

CONTRIBUTING FACTORS

In my work with clients who have gender issues, I have identified nine factors that may contribute to transgendered behavior, without being its sole cause. I put each factor in the form of a question and then give a composite of the type of client dealing with this particular contributing factor. It would be helpful both to you and your client to explore these factors and see what holds true for him.

1.   *Was there a prenatal development that determined either a clear or confused gender consciousness?*
        Example: "This has been a part of me for as long as I can remember. I thought when I got older that I might be a homosexual, but I wasn't attracted to men. I always wanted to be with girls. And later I envied them and wanted to be like them."

2.   *Is there a phobic response to the imagined or real violence of male authority figures and/or the male part of oneself?*
        Example: "I'm afraid of men. I've always been uncomfortable around them and what they're capable of, their brutishness and their violence. My father was brutal to me and I was abused as a child by men, also by other boys. As a woman I don't have those feelings, but as a man I'm afraid of what I'm capable of."

3.   *Is it like an addiction, in that it masks pain and deprivation, similar to drugs, alcohol, or compulsive sex?*

Example: "When I put the clothes on, I can relax and all my troubles disappear. It's my greatest pleasure and it's been the source for strong erotic feelings that help me forget the weight of my obligations."

4. *Is it a conditioned response built up over time from the positive and erotic feelings associated with the crossdressing?*

    Example: "The first time I did it, I had such wonderful feelings that I wanted to do it more and more and kept going back to it."

    Pleasure is a very strong conditioner, and once we find something that is really pleasurable to the organism, we want to keep repeating it; but, as has been indicated earlier, there must be a pre-disposition to it for the behavior to catch on.

5. *Is it a creative way of attempting to resolve the old Oedipal complex?*

    Example: "I have always adored women, starting with my mother. I was aroused by wearing her clothes, but she's safe from me sexually if we are both girls. It's a way of feeling close to her without breaking any rules or getting in trouble with my father."

6. *Is it an advanced form of narcissism (i.e. excessive love or admiration for oneself or erotic pleasure derived from regarding one's body image)?*

    Example: "I've created a feminine persona that the male side of me responds to more strongly than to any real woman. I fall in love with her in the mirror or in photographs. I love taking lots and lots of pictures of myself and giving them out to people."

7. *Is it a replacement for a loveless, sexless relationship that is perpetuated out of fear of facing the truth and moving on? Or for the lack of an intimate relationship in which one has a joyful sense of one's maleness?*

    Example: "When I was with my former wife, the only way I could feel sexually aroused was to dress or imagine myself dressed when I was with her. Since I have been with my new partner, who is very sexual, attractive, and loving, my need to dress has almost disappeared."

8. *Is it a displacement of the feminine soul inside all men that needs to be related to internally, but instead is given external trappings and confused with the real internal relationship?*

    Example: "Since I've been in active dialogue with my inner ideal woman's soul and feel in constant contact with her, my desire to dress has diminished."

9. *Is it allowing the expression of an artistic soul who beautifies his person for aesthetic satisfaction the way an artist might with other materials and spaces?*

    Example: "I enjoy being creative with visual media in whatever way I can. Women can be more colorful than men in our society. I like the drama of it." (Michael Jackson might be an example of this.)

This list of factors is not exhaustive, and many of them may overlap. Also, at different times in the person's experience, different factors may come into play. The important point is for you and your client to find out as much as you can about what affects his experience.

CHAPTER 5

PROBLEM AREAS

Unhealthy and Destructive Patterns

It is important to distinguish between people who have serious problems which they need to work on despite their gender identity challenges, and people who are involved in unhealthy or even destructive behaviors related to their gender expression.

There are a number of signs that indicate when crossdressing behavior is destructive:

- When he is unable to reveal it to his closest peers and it is surrounded by feelings of shame and guilt.

- When it interferes with intimacy (emotional or sexual) with a partner.

- When it is his only stress outlet and he feels compelled to turn to the behavior without feeling as though he has a choice.

- When it leads to lying, stealing, antisocial, or exclusively autoerotic behavior, or when it is accompanied by substance abuse.

- When he is angry with himself about it.

- When he has not learned to manage it with the rest of his life and give it a realistic priority in line with his life goals.

For instance, if he is obsessing about dressing while he is working or playing a sport, then he is not in control.

- When his self-esteem as a man is so poor that he escapes from doing something about *that* by pouring all his admiration for himself into the femme expression.

- When he is dishonest with himself and others about its importance to him.

When these feelings or behaviors show up in the counseling situation, they provide guidance to the counselor about the direction of the work.

There are also other obviously unhealthy patterns which may not be related to gender expression. If a person is really dysfunctional in his life (can't hold a job, for example, or has a very short attention span, is sullen or depressed most of the time, or has psychosomatic ailments), you know there are problems to be addressed. You must deal with these problems just as you would with anyone who comes into counseling.

If these phenomena exist and a person is trying to deal with gender expression, they have to be dealt with in and of themselves, often first.

If a person is chronically angry or hostile, for instance, and feels victimized by things external to himself, then that is the process to be addressed. He can be helped to see he has a problem which doesn't necessarily have to do with gender confusion. He will be better able to address his gender issues when his life is working more smoothly and he feels good about himself. He may try to blame everything on his gender issues, but you can point out there are many gender confused persons who are fully functional as parents, artists or whatever constitutes their life pursuits.

Learning to Cope

Often, early in the counseling process, we discover the client comes from a severely dysfunctional family. I have had many gender clients from alcoholic homes, from homes where there was some kind of battering, or from homes with incest. There may be other kinds of sexual acting out, or compulsive gambling, or drugs.

Psychotherapy needs to be done with these clients. They can look back at their primary family situations and access feelings long denied or learn how they were affected by the disorder around them.

This information comes out when childhood is discussed. An exploration of coping mechanisms will ensue.

One from an alcoholic family, for example, has grown up in a world of denial. The alcoholic is often surrounded by enablers. They aid and abet the alcoholic in staying the way he or she is.

The young child learns to suppress important issues. The family can't deal with pain and can't challenge it. A child from such a family will not be able to talk about either crossdressing behavior or transsexual feelings. This family doesn't want to talk about difficult subjects. They would rather pretend that everything is OK, or possibly drink their problems away.

People from dysfunctional families often want to be secretive, to lie about their activities in order to protect themselves from any kind of irrational responses or questioning that they feel they are unable to handle.

A "T" who has been abused as a child may have serious complications in dealing with a spouse or partner because he fully expects to be punished in some way. He is likely to project all kinds of harsh responses on the partner, which might or might not be how the partner is actually going to respond if gender issues are discussed.

Just as a child often leaves a trail to try to unconsciously alert parents that something is troubling him, a "T" might leave a false fingernail or an article of clothing around or not put something back exactly the way it was. The wife discovers it and then the issue comes out.

Another factor often emerging is that the "T" cannot stand living with duplicity. Trying to keep crossdressing hidden is often more painful than whatever imagined consequences might occur if it were revealed. Some people get to the point of desperation where they absolutely <u>have</u> to tell their significant other about their behavior. They feel that the psychic hell they're in from keeping their feelings inside is much worse than any problems that might result from such a discussion, even if it means losing the marriage.

Dysfunctional patterns learned in the family and other places are brought into the current situation and affect the way a person deals with the gender issue. But they usually don't have to do with the actual gender behavior itself. There are many happily raised people from the gender community who crossdress or are transsexual, and there are others who come from miserable backgrounds. Family history may be a contributing factor, but not a sole cause of these behaviors. However, family behavior patterns can certainly influence how "T"s respond to their condition and their world.

Facing Loss and Grief

This population of clients, more than most others, are faced with many possible losses in their lives.

The crossdresser may have to deal with his wife's repulsion, loss of romantic feeling, loss of admiration, loss of trust, loss of sexual activity and more.

The transsexual stands to lose the whole relationship, the marriage, for sure, in its original form. She may have rifts with her children who feel protective of their mother and angry with the transsexual for changing their lives and not being their recognizable daddy any more. She will lose her physical strength and will often not have the same work and income opportunities she did as a man.

The wife grieves the loss of the man to whom she was originally attracted, and has to give up many of her beliefs and suppositions about this person, whom she thought she knew inside and out.

It is important for you to help these clients face their losses and grieve them. Often, the sadness and disappointment is overwhelming. But it is an important part of the process of forging a direction which will work for each of them in the future.

PART II

THE COUNSELOR'S PROCESS

KNOW THYSELF

KNOW THY CLIENT

Alice: (referring to mustard)..."It's a vegetable. It doesn't look like one but it is."

"I quite agree with you" said the Duchess; "and the moral of that is Be what you would seem to be---or, if you'd like it put more simply---'Never imagine yourself not to be otherwise than what it might appear to others that what you were or might have been was not otherwise than what you had been would have appeared to them to be otherwise.'"

From "Alice in Wonderland"
Lewis Carroll

INTRODUCTION

Gender counseling is a dynamic process.

We need to take into account not only all the things the client says about his gender expression and gender experience, but we also have to pay attention to the resources of each client.

How does this person access and express information?

Is he visual, auditory, physical, emotional, intellectual?

What is this person's body language?

What was his past and his family of origin?

We must be able to separate the dysfunctions in the family in which he was raised from anything that is currently happening with his gender expression, and not lump it all into one big dysfunction.

Of equal importance is knowing your own resources, blind spots and gender issues and learning how to use them creatively in your work with clients. See the questions for you to reflect on at the end of this chapter.

The counseling job is much more difficult if many of your own issues have not been recognized and worked out. This is particularly pertinent in dealing with gender issues. It is my opinion that any counselor, in particular, one who is going to be dealing with gender issues with a client, should work through his or her own sex and gender issues first.

You, as a gender identity counselor, help bring about insight and personal development in both yourself and your client.

This, in turn, has a positive impact on a society needing to learn how to embrace diversity and feel at home in a multi-gendered world.

CHAPTER 1

THE COUNSELOR PREPARES

I will be addressing you as though you are new to counseling in order to make certain points--even though I realize that many of you reading this book may have many years of practice.

The Centered Counselor

Unless the counselor is personally centered, not much additional centering can happen on a significant level in the counseling relationship.

Being centered means that you are fully present, you are not preoccupied with your own concerns or anything outside that counseling session. You are open to whatever comes, and are prepared to respond to it as honestly and openly as you can. You have a sense, let's say, of a spiritual dimension--that this entire process is for a higher good that goes beyond either one of you, that you are helping humanity by working at the frontiers of identity and consciousness.

Whatever improvement in centering takes place in yourself or your client, you can expect the results are going to be spread to other people.

Body Mind Awareness

As a counselor, you need to have a way of being enough in touch with your own body and mind so that you recognize something happening, you are remembering to breathe, you are remembering to support your weight in the chair. You are always remembering that you're _there_, no matter what's coming toward you from the client's side of the dialogue.

No One Right Way

You're also there supporting the client's ability to solve his own issue, rather than doing it for him.

There is no one right way to counsel people.

The art of good counseling is to have a sense of what's likely to be productive in the moment in the larger context of the client's ongoing process.

As you gain more and more experience, a paradox reveals itself. You see what clients have in common wherever they are along the gender spectrum: they are living in a basically hostile world environment. Anyone who lives in a hostile or rigid environment is going to have problems with identity.

There are as many differences as there are people. It is why we must pay attention to this particular person, and not generalize or try to categorize.

We don't want to fall into the mistake that Kate Bornstein speaks about so beautifully in her book, *Gender Outlaw*, of having to pigeonhole people and be in a closed, static system rather than a dynamic one.

Dealing With Feelings

People with gender issues bring beliefs and assumptions about themselves to counseling that they've absorbed from the culture and their families. It helps to enable them to look at all of these, then work themselves back to *tabula rasa*, a clean slate, so they can write their own story.

They need to learn how to become aware of their feelings, to accept them, to be able to name them, and finally to act on them. A lot of clients, especially at the beginning of therapy, can't do that. They weren't taught how to deal with feelings in school (and probably not at home, either). It helps a lot if counselors can model the acknowledgment and expression of feelings.

Feelings are truths to be considered as people make decisions. They are not to be discounted; they are just as important as thoughts.

Clients need to understand that feelings exist in their bodies, not just in their minds. They can learn where anger, fear and sadness exist by referring to the sensations in their bodies. They need to be able to look at, and move through, their fears and hesitations.

It's not comfortable for a lot of people to stay in present time, paying attention to what's going on inside them. They can learn to bear some discomfort when they're asked to examine their feelings or their reactions to certain statements I may make, or to disturbing thoughts they may be having at the moment. If they practice these skills, they can begin to feel more in control of their lives and more fully alive.

Achieving Balance

Most of us are unbalanced; for instance, we work too hard, or we feel inferior, or we are antisocial. We worry too much about some things and don't pay enough attention to other things. In our work we may be one way; for example, very organized, methodical, and attentive to details. At home that may all change; things may be a mess.

So during the learning and consulting process we ask: How can you be the most balanced person possible? What's underdeveloped? What's overdeveloped? To what do you need to pay attention?

Balance can be brought about a number of ways. Learning to meditate is helpful. Applying models of what we do well in one situation to others where we feel less effective can also help.

Often, crossdressing clients will say that one persona is level-headed and well organized, and the other is "loosy goosy" or flamboyant or passive. (It can be either the masculine or femme side for either behavior set.)

Achieving balance may involve having each side counsel the other and reach agreement about when it is appropriate to be which way. This helps the person feel more integrated and in control.

Avoiding the "Rescue" Trap

A trap you might fall into is to try to rescue the client so as not to feel your <u>own</u> discomfort. Your actions may not benefit the client whose process gets interrupted.

If, for instance, a client is talking about how s/he felt very frightened talking to a close friend about his/her gender expression, and s/he starts crying or is visibly shaken, it doesn't help to tell her, "Everything is going to be all right, and you did the right thing," or other consoling words.

Here is an opportunity for the client and the counselor to be able to look at and try to understand the depth of that feeling, to consider the risk involved by the "T" in talking to someone they've known all their lives in some other context.

An empathic statement might be in order, such as "That must have been a very difficult thing for you to do."

If you are uncomfortable with tears or have been conditioned to "smooth things over," then your reaction is going to be to try to help that person to feel better at that moment. Solace may actually be counter-productive. The situation may elicit something like a parent's response to an upset child, instead of a more productive, compassionate interaction between two adults.

Some persons have been so conditioned to keep their feelings inside that it's a major victory for them if their eyes even water.

Others are much more labile and will easily cry. Emotional release often has to do with the personality of the client, not the kind of problem. In order to allow strong emotions in the client, the counselor needs to work on his or her <u>own</u> comfort level with the expression of strong feelings. In gender work, feelings are particularly strong.

Time after time, clients have told me that being listened to in a non-judgmental way, and having the counselor be present and actively engaged in the process was instrumental in producing healing or feelings of self-esteem and well-being.

The Ebb and Flow of Contact

In a good helping relationship a natural rhythm develops between the counselor and the client.

This natural rhythm is like the rhythm of the ocean. The client comes out toward the counselor. The counselor comes out toward the client. Each of them also come back to themselves.

It is lovely when that rhythm works well, because it feels like a dance.

Self Reflection for the Counselor

In your effort to be as aware as possible of your own responses and conditioning about gender identity, take some time to ponder these questions.

1. How did you discover your gender?

2. How did you feel about it? Has it changed, gone through stages?

3. How did you feel the first time you encountered a biological male presenting as a woman?

4. What is your response to masculine women?

5. Along the gender spectrum what attracts/repels you?

6. What do you imagine would be the most difficult aspect of gender identity work for you? What is there about that which relates to something unexplored in you?

7. Is there any way in which you experience differences between your head and your heart in this matter?

8. In what ways have you experimented with your own gender presentation? If not, why not? If so, what did you feel?

9. If you have a partner, how would you react to him/her telling you they wanted to adopt the opposite gender role?

10. Can you recall dreams or fantasies in which you switched gender, or someone close to you did? (See section on dreams in Chapter 3.)

CHAPTER 2

CLIENT PATTERNS

In my work with transgendered clients, I have recognized a number of non-helpful patterns of behavior on the part of the client which need to be addressed.

- **Starting with a symptom or a solution** instead of with a problem. For instance: "There is no point in dressing if I can't look right." Or: "I am never going to tell anyone about this because no one would understand." Or: "My wife hates my crossdressing, so I guess we'll have to split up." Comments like these indicate that the person is jumping to a conclusion before the problem is even analyzed.

- **Inability to move to anything beyond the superficial level**. This type of person sounds like a broken record, repeating the same things over and over. Or the person won't even discuss his feelings: "I just want hormones and I'll be happy."

- **Being too task-oriented**: "As long as I have an action plan and follow it, I won't have a problem."

- **Being too process-oriented.** This person can only address feelings; he is a big feeling machine who won't do anything about the way he is feeling, immobilizing himself out of fear.

Such a person might be afraid of hurting others through his decisions, so he does nothing. This problem comes up often with gender-conflicted clients. The person may keep crossdressing a secret based on the fear that his wife will be hurt, or won't be able to handle his or her feelings or actions.

A person can be afraid of feelings; of new behavior; of being dependent; of being independent; of not being in control; or of committing oneself to a plan, a person, or an action.

- **Clowning**. The client may make fun of and discount his or her own problems or other people's problems. The positive aspect of humor, which often helps people get through problems, become distorted; the humor becomes a weapon used to belittle oneself and one's feelings.

- **Being mistrustful**. The client may blame others for his problems or discomforts, be cynical, or even be paranoid, feeling that people are out to get him.

  Other characteristics include withdrawing, shutting down, projecting (assuming that other people have feelings or thoughts they may not have or that he himself has), and playing games of manipulation.

  A person with a deep degree of mistrust tries to assert control by avoiding certain tasks or certain situations, discounting, making things unimportant, pouting, or being vindictive.

  If you see any of these kinds of behaviors in the client, you know there is a trust issue, and that is the area to work on. If the general feelings of mistrust are exaggerated, generalized, and fairly unremitting, then the client may have a more serious disturbance and may need to be seen by someone well-versed in serious mental conditions quite separate from the gender issue.

A mistrustful person will also doubt the efficacy of the counseling process itself. She didn't really come in here, the transsexual says, of her own free will but because it's required by the Benjamin Standards of Care.* She has to fulfill the requirement without really trusting the process. She is mistrustful of society.

A lot of the feelings that people have about society are borne out by the way society responds.

However, society is changed by people who trust themselves enough to <u>be</u> who they feel they are; who can be friendly, willing to engage in conversations, ask questions, and not run away because they don't trust themselves to deal with present situations.

- **Generalizing**. The person speaks about "you" instead of "I," such as using "you" in general about people, or "it," or "everybody." He may say that "everybody" worries about such and such, without really being self-referential. He refuses to be in present time, talks of the past or the future, theorizes, talks in platitudes, and is vague or irrelevant.

- **Projecting**. It is important to teach the client that one's greatest teachers are often those who most stir up one's most negative responses or fear responses. This allows you to reframe the experience of fear to that of curiosity.

*See Appendix

Suppose a crossdresser goes to a mall, someone looks at him sideways, and he gets terrified. What can <u>he</u> learn from that experience about how to handle it next time, how to talk to himself about it, what to do about various situations that he might come across in his life, so that he can be comfortable and have a plan for how he wants to deal with these uncomfortable experiences?

If you perceive that the client has a fixed eye focus, or is looking all over the place, then it is important to bring that fact to his attention and find out what is going on.

I've had clients who have been afraid to make eye contact with me; their eyes dart around the room or they look down at the floor while, at the same time, telling me the most personal, intimate things.

I explain to them that I am greatly interested in what they are telling me, but I am also noticing that I'm not being looked at. I might ask them what kind of feeling they have about looking at me and talking to me at the same time. "Let's experiment with that. Let's learn what's going on here."

This type of intervention often leads to the uncovering of feelings of shame, of guilt, or the fear of seeing disapproval on the counselor's face (the projection).

You might give the client permission to not look at you at all, but stay aware of his feelings as he talks. Big changes happen, because then you can work on the shame-based feelings and you can bring some humor into it.

You can tell the client to take peeks at you every once in awhile, and notice when the eye contact becomes more frequent.

You can even make some suggestions: "You seem to be getting more comfortable; I noticed each look is a little longer; that's great."

You can positively reinforce the behavior that they are trying to develop. On the other hand, they may really want to focus on their inner experience, in which case you can encourage them to "stay inside" and come out when they are ready.

In working with projections it is also important to explore how the client might be unconscious about feelings toward you, i.e., "are there ways you disapprove of me, don't like what I'm saying or doing?" You can invite the client to bring out these feelings, if they exist.

Full exploration about projections can help build trust and safety in your relationship with the gender client.

CHAPTER 3

THE COUNSELOR'S TOOLKIT:

Sensory and Experiential Process

A wealth of information is available to you beyond the actual content of the client's verbal message about his situation. This can evidence itself in body language, images and projections, voice quality and speech patterns, metaphors and all kinds of distractions and associations (like one client who, while telling me there were no problems between him and his mother, was rubbing out an ant on the floor).

Vital to the counseling process is your responsibility to honor as much of this material as you can identify; it is just as important as what the client is saying outright about his situation.

This is where you can be tremendously creative in developing ways to increase your range of observation skills. You can get out of the rut of relying totally on verbal exchange and, instead, take a more holistic approach. It's also more fun. Of course, it requires that you become comfortable with a wider range of self-expression than you have been used to in your counseling practice. But the rewards can be highly satisfying.

Identifying these other forms of expression can be especially useful with gender-exploring clients who are trying to live out both their masculine and feminine aspect and need as wide a range of safe ways of self-expression as can be suggested and encouraged.

There are five areas of such information which can enrich your work with gender clients. (The bibliography will list some books which can aid you in a more in-depth exploration.)

- Visual information (Imagery and Dream Work)
- Auditory information
- Body signals
- Tactile experience
- Polarities

Visual Information
Imagery

You may observe that you are working with a client who expresses himself visually a lot of the time. He will say things like, "I see...I notice...This problem is hard to look at...I can't see what this has to do with..."

You might ask him to close his eyes and get a picture of what he is expressing. He can then draw it or describe it to you. Make it clear that it doesn't matter what the drawing looks like; it's the process of expressing himself that is important. You both then have something to focus on (another visual phrase!) and may become aware that you can get information this way which might not emerge by simply conversing.

A crossdresser might be encouraged to draw an idealized image of his femme self, or bring in photos or pictures from magazines from which he can make a collage. Someone in transition can be encouraged to produce drawings or collages which express what her life as a woman might be like.

You can ask clients to describe scenes from movies or plays they have seen. Or shop windows. Or catalogues. You get the idea--any visual images which evoke feeling. Thus you develop a springboard for delving more deeply into their experience of themselves, plus you discover more information about their self-image.

Dream Work Methods

In the visual channel, exploring dreams has been a major tool in counseling my clients and being aware of my own process. I have followed not only their dreams, but my own, including fantasy material.

At first, clients are often resistant to exploring dreams, a mixture of effrontery to their rational minds which says, "How can pictures I see in my sleep possibly have any meaning?" and fear of what they might find out by actually investigating this material. Often, once they begin to bring their dreams into the counseling process, they become quite interested in what they discover.

The **benefits** of working with your "T" client's dreams include:

- Recognizing important parts of the self which are dissociated

- Getting a reading of where the "T" is in his process

- Receiving guidance for you regarding what needs attention or expression

- Uncovering unfinished business

- Getting practical help with issues in everyday life

- Broadening the possibilities of areas to explore

- Freeing the imagination, soul and spirit to express itself

The **benefits** of working with your own transgendered dreams include:

- Gaining understanding of your own hidden feelings about this phenomenon and specific clients or issues

- Having insights about what might be helpful interventions

- Gaining empathy with states of being that are usual for your clients but may not be part of your ordinary reality

- Enhancing your own personal and spiritual growth

Gestalt methods of working with dreams: (examples of interventions)
- Become each person or object in the dreams. Describe yourself and your function. Listen for existential messages.

- Have dialogues between different entities or between yourself and any part.

- Tell the dream from the point of view of another figure in the dream, including inanimate objects.

- Draw images and say what you see.

- Be aware of feelings in your body as you tell the dream. Amplify them and let them "speak" to you.

- Connect the dream material to your current life experience.

Jungian Methods (acknowledgment to Robert Johnson's *Inner Work* for some of the ideas presented here)

- Focus on each image in the dream. Free associate to it (plays on words, myths, metaphors, song, etc). Notice the energy it has for you, feelings it stimulates.

- Connect dream image to your inner life by asking questions such as "What part of me is that? How is it like me/what are its main characteristics?"

- Is there a guide of any sort showing you the way? It could be an animal, a train conductor, a shopkeeper. What are you being shown or advised to do?

- What is the essential message of the dream? Look for an interpretation that shows you something you were not aware of.

- Honor the dream. Find a way to "let the dream know you have heard it." This could be as simple as lighting a candle and saying thank you, to actually acting on the guidance you have received.

There are many books available which will give you more detailed information on working with dreams. Some of my favorites are listed in the bibliography.

Fantasy

If your client has trouble remembering his dreams, you might ask him to share a fantasy, or guide him in one which is not too specific. An example would be "You are in a hallway standing in front of a door to a room you have never been in. Open the door, enter the room and explore what is there." The material from the fantasy can be worked on exactly the same way as the dream material.

***

Polygendered persons have vivid imaginations. It can be said that they had to be able to fantasize and dream in order to survive in a world which has resistance to allowing them full expression. It is also a great resource in the counseling process for bringing out different aspects of the self. Some clients have spent most of their time in their fantasy world before they get to you. They are looking to you to make it all right for them to own and manifest their inner feelings and fantasies about who they really are. You are in a position to help free your client's spirit and thereby promote healing and integration in a formerly fragmented person.

DREAMS OF A COUNSELOR

I am including some of the many transgendered dreams I have had since I began this work so you can see their value in presenting issues needing to be worked on as a gender counselor. The comments are not intended to be comprehensive, but merely to indicate one or two major issues brought to the foreground for my reflection. They might also help you to recognize what might be useful to pay attention to in your own dreams.

1983 (during the first year of my work with "T"s)

I am a male. I meet a beautiful, fun blond female who turns out to be the new domestic helper in my parents' house.

> *Commentary: My newly acknowledged fantasy of what it would look like to be the opposite sex gets a chance to manifest in this dream. My inner parents are the union of masculine and feminine. In real life, I am more at home with my masculine side. The "domestic helper" is my less known beguiling feminine side being playful and welcoming us to unite. My work with males who adore the feminine bring this need for my own integration to the surface.*

1985

I go to the ladies room. There's a man in there who is changing from having been crossdressed. I tell him he's in the wrong room and ask him to leave. He bugs me, keeps hanging around, talking to me. I want privacy. I've brought a newspaper. I'm going to sit in the stall and read while I "go." I don't feel comfortable until he gets out. He doesn't. Finally after I tell him, very forcibly to get out, he does. But even after he leaves, I position myself in the booth so he couldn't possibly see me even if he were looking through the door.

> *Commentary: I am uncomfortable with the crossdresser entering my private space. I don't want him to bug me, and need to clearly establish my boundaries. I have to ask myself the question. "In what circumstance and under what conditions must I separate my private life from the social side of this work?"*

1986

A group of crossdressed men come wandering into a space I'm in. I ask them if they are crossdressers. They say "yes." I tell them (as others come in) that I happen to be the only humanistic psychologist I know who serves this community. The room is now full of crossdressers. I say I will give them 15 minutes free but then would have to charge them. On second thought, I say, everyone pay a dollar. I go up and down the rows collecting the money. It gets mixed up with the money of colleagues who own the building. I have to make change. I am confused. I ask someone to help.

> *Commentary: Another boundary dream. What do I freely give to this client community and what do I charge for? How does my contracting have to be different from that of my colleagues? What do I owe them? What "change" do I need to make? What is my value to them and theirs to me?*

1988

Twins. One is a female-to-male transsexual and now has male pattern baldness. The other sister is crossdressed as a man but has a full head of hair.

Commentary: Integration of sex and gender elements is starting to take place in my psyche but is still individualized.

My daughter appears with a beard. I am slightly shocked, but accepting.

Commentary: Could I accept this in a family member? I guess so!

1994 (right after Fantasia Fair)

I walk in on my mother as she is drying herself from a shower. I see that she has a penis. Her big secret is out. She is a full blown hermaphrodite. She says she didn't want to tell me; it would cause confusion. She doesn't want to talk about it. I am very curious.

Merissa (a community leader who recently underwent SRS) tells me she'll have to go into disguise for a little while as a man.

Commentary: I am more ready to acknowledge the existence of all sex and gender within me. I also recognize that society expects us to conform to its expectations about our roles so we all disguise ourselves from time to time. The dream asks me to investigate what I want to hide and what I want to reveal. It presents a comprehensive symbol, both personal and collective, i.e. the hermaphrodite; she who birthed me.

Counselors, my suggestion to you is to begin to keep a dream journal if you do not already do so. Pay special attention to dreams referring to sex and gender. They can give you invaluable information and guidance about your own process, both personally and professionally.

DREAMS OF A CROSSDRESSER

1. Bill
(actually two dreams...separate but in the same evening...)

I am crossdressed, in a beautiful mansion, as the guest of crossdressers. It has a large inside, beautiful decor, and we are all relaxing, having tea or coffee, as women friends would do. We look around at the decor...admire the paintings and the bric-a-brac...being ourselves and admiring one another.

I feel relaxed, and in the femme mode, feeling as I should, enjoying my crossdressing and looking/being a woman...I am seated on a large beautiful sofa, chatting with another crossdresser seated at the opposite end of the sofa. She is wearing a simple skirt, and a sweater, light in color, brocaded with patterns in such a lovely design...and with jewelry...simple, but very nice...I feel warmth, friendliness, and admire her "look"... We feel relaxed, a mutual accepting and are enjoying ourselves together.

We look around the place, curious, admiring, gossiping about it. Then I go to sit down again on the sofa. There are other people around. I hear a man sneeze behind me, behind the sofa, and some of it sprays over me on the head. I am disgusted by this! How rude, and slovenly! Why is he doing that to me--on purpose? It seems so...because I catch a glance as he walks by and he looks at me with a smirk on his face...as if he did it on purpose...Why? Why should he pick on me? It's like a bully would act. I think I see a woman with him, perhaps his wife...I get the impression that they are leaving, having seen enough of us, that they are uneasy about the scene there...

Commentary: Who is the unrecognized "bully" that lives inside the dreamer? The slovenly male, the refined woman--inner aspects--how can they relate?

2.

I am on the telephone, in the middle of a conversation with the owner of Vernon's, a specialty boutique catering to the crossdressing community, in Waltham, Massachusetts. (I had met him in real life, over 4 years ago, dressing in his store basement.) We chat a little, in a friendly way. I am not anxious. He says something like: "Yes, we are having an event here (for crossdressers). Everyone will be here...why don't you come... M. will be there." (M. is in my gender therapy group, I know her well and think she is very feminine.)

I feel a deep connection in this dream, a deep feeling. I feel drawn to the dream, of being invited to cross over into another world...

Commentary: The dreamer reveals his deep attraction to the feminine and his desire to be part of that community.

3.

I am looking in the suitcase in my bedroom where I keep some women' clothes handy. I am going through the items when I take out a bra one time, then another bra another time, seeing that they are not my bras! I realize they are L's! How did they get in here? She has left stuff at my place before, but with my women's clothes? She would have to know that these are mine and suspect that I crossdress! But she never told me that she did that or know anything about my desires...

Commentary: The dream asks the dreamer to investigate how much he is willing to reveal about his crossdressing desires to the women in his life. How will knowing this affect their feeling for him? He evidences anxiety about being discovered. If this happens in real life, how does he want to handle it?

DREAMS OF TRANSSEXUALS

Jamie (also see "PERSONAL HISTORY," PART IV)

These dreams are chronological and give some sense of progress.

- Preparing to take a rocket to another planet. Trip guide says, "Before you go there are a lot of things you need to take care of here on earth to prepare for the trip."

   Commentary: This was a pivotal dream which indicated both to the male-to-woman client and to me that, indeed, she was headed for transition but realized that she had a lot of work to do before she was ready to go.

- Woman surgeon examining dreamer's genitals prepares for SRS surgery. J is wide awake. Surgeon says, "They haven't prepared you yet."

   Commentary: Another dream later on in transition, which clearly states that she is aware she is not ready yet for surgery.

- J is watching an actor playing a sage from the past. He was explaining why he had SRS, portrayed by male actor. Dreamer's feeling: Wow! One of the great men had no qualm...

   Commentary: We can see how the client is getting herself ready psychologically.

- Dad finds out about J's transgenderism and yells at him. J says, "I finally found my life and I'm not going to let you take it away."

  Commentary: Important declaration to all who disapprove, including an inner father figure.

- J going somewhere with mother. J has short blond hair, thinks, "You look great!"

  Commentary: A positive feminine self-image.

Stephanie (also see "PERSONAL HISTORY," PART IV)

Stephanie (one month into therapy)
- I'm sitting in car with intelligence agent (I'm a woman). In Beirut. Car pulls up. Someone says, "Pass the parcel, honey." He hands it over. Car explodes in a few blocks. He and agent in hospital building. Driver of other car there, says, "I thought you were dead." I say, "I was supposed to be." He pulls a weapon. Stephanie runs, is chased upstairs. Boy standing near them, runs into plant with S. Heating vent, air conditioning plant. Hot pipes. Lose track of boy. Run out. Shriek for help to attract driver' attention. S. picks up length of pipe and swings. Wakes up.

- Should I wear paisley or houndstooth dress?

- Inspecting emissions control in plant. I should have worn something else besides navy dress and heels.

- Day after holiday in Brattleboro. Has jeans on under dress. Airport. Rental plane like Vespa motor scooter (no starter). Pull propeller to start. Middle and ring finger cut to bone. Blood. Scream for help. Call rescue. Bandage. Hold injured hand over head. Hold bandage. Squeeze pressure point. Call parents. Ask for Mark, Robin (siblings). Change of clothes. Crying. Guys embarrassed (S. is a woman). Losing strength. M and R at hospital. Steph motions to Robin in private, says, "If I die, find head of emergency and kill him."

   Commentary: Life and death issues of identity and survival strongly stated in images. Pay attention to themes of wounding, fear of being hurt, cry for help.

November, 1994 (2 years later)--Shortly after this, Stephanie successfully completes her SRS and her counseling.)

Seppuku--Japanese suicide involving two persons

- S. is male self kneeling on floor on a woven rice mat in a stark room. Someone is standing behind him. S. has both a long and a short sword. S. hands long sword to this person and says: "After this is over, these are yours" (meaning swords). S. uses short sword to cut his belly. "Now" he gasps. The person behind him cuts his head off. Now he becomes the one behind him who is a woman.

   Commentary: Notice the ritualistic ceremony as an expression of transition. Explore and acknowledge the new woman's power.

81

PRE-OPERATIVE TRANSSEXUAL (near beginning of counseling)

Marie, 1991

1. I am with two people: B., my boss (she' strong, I admire her, androgynous, she took another job with female boss who could be a transsexual) and T., my best friend, male.

I am going to his house (don't know why). I knock, door opens, I see B. dressed in S & M dominatrix outfit. T. is shorter, in front of her in femme camisole (baby doll). I'm shocked they're together, that he is wearing femme clothes, that there is relationship. They act nonchalant, like it's normal for them to be together like this and to accept people into their home. It felt normal, not like he was going to be made part of a kinky scene.

2. I'm a character seeing the world. I know I'm not real. San Francisco environment. Landscapes and objects not real. Fear in the beings around me (I've been dropped into this place).

3. Ceremony. Throngs. Very formal. Guards, other worldly, like Mayan. Raised areas, high priestesses. Great Being going to come. Dark Creature Being comes to front of altar. Appearance of mutants like Ninja Turtles. Special effects but not cartoonish. Great fearsome head. He is raging mad. As he gets angrier, he changes. Something starts growing, it gets bigger and barbed. The growth curves, penetrates the urn and shatters it, i.e. broke a hole through it. Giant member. It (he) is cooked in front of us, creature in great agony. The meal separates from his body. He's left with a stump.

4. On Columbus expedition to America. Different views of the harbor and ships. Gets on the ship, encounters really rough water. (At first, the ship is tied up, then free, they have to tie it up but it's difficult; they have to keep ship next to the pier, a balancing act.)

We land with Columbus, tropical lagoon. Columbus is mystified at lack of cities and people. I'm standing across lagoon watching him. Car appears behind him and disappears. I wander up in hills with a woman, see horses, joyful, running. Are they from ship or the land, and who are the people riding them?

Hills covered with vegetation, look natural, but they're really the ends of something, a front; like canyons that have been cut out of a bluff. It's sunset. Now I'm curious about what's going on. Suddenly, vistas open. I see an incredible cut in the canyon-- an Indiana Jones scene, living things down there, horses, full of them. These horses are being hidden from view, not like other horses. Richness, something here. If I walked to the end of that canyon it would open into a plateau. I walked in, it narrowed. There's a gale, an ebony screen: only one person can get by.

Turns out to be an entrance to a grotto-style restaurant/club. Cave-like place. Glass wall, spiral staircase upwards. Big tables all around, wing back chairs, big panelling, prints. People look strange. I had feeling I didn't belong.

Said to a woman, "Why didn't you tell me there were people here?" Native Americans dressed in traditional western suits. Women in formal clothing. Proper. We're out of place even though from a superior culture. They ignore us after seeing us.

But maitre d' bouncer confronts us, begins to restrain us, capture us. This scares me, he tries to reveal me, grabbing at my skin to reveal Indian face he expects to see. We push him. He falls through glass wall and is gone.

They become a mob. We run to escape. I have to get back to the lagoon. (Dream ends)

(Continued in fantasy): Maze between me and lagoon. Gate, hallway, rooms, isn't this marvelous? Finally, they had to eliminate us to preserve their world. Oh my God! I don't remember how we got here. Eventually we are caught, put on display, inevitability of the new culture overpowering the natives.

Commentary: Marie has elaborate, mythical-type dreams with rich imagery bringing in history, exotic locales, and archetypes. Work with the metaphors, association and personal responses to this material.

Pay attention to all the guidance available for the client's real-life journey.

***

A separate book could be written on transgender dreams. My purpose in including these examples is to give you a sense of the richness of material available to you which can help you sort out both your feelings and those of your client. The dreams can give you excellent clues as to where the process is currently and where it is heading. Many clients who have never paid attention to their dreams before begin to appreciate their inner creativity in an entirely new way!

Auditory Information

Pay attention not only to what the client is saying but how she is saying it. Is she rushing to get the words out? Is she hesitating after every word or constantly correcting herself? Is she speaking inaudibly or shouting? Is she interrupting every time you try to say something?

If her behavior is consistent, you might try to explore the feeling behind it, then experiment with having her do the opposite and see what happens. Often, feelings of anxiety, inadequacy, or hostility become clear once these patterns are examined.

The content can be explored not only for what is consciously being expressed but for the poetic metaphors (I feel like I'm in a cage), the persistent use of hyperbole (women are totally wonderful, gorgeous creatures), strange expressions or sounds made (remember Al Pacino's blind soldier character in *Scent of a Woman*, who makes the braying sound?).

Sometimes a client has a strong reaction to something that the counselor says. A variety of surprising feelings may emerge.

Recently one of my clients was talking about getting her name changed, and how that action has produced an experience of identity which hadn't existed before (even though she has been working on her transsexuality.)

Then I asked her to imagine, for instance, what she would do if someone tried to ridicule her, or pick a fight with her. How would she respond in her new role?

She went completely blank because she realized, "Oh my God, in my former role, I would have said that I would knock the guy down!"

"But suddenly I'm realizing I'm a different person. As this person I am not somebody who likes fighting. I'm actually afraid of it. I guess I'd look for the nearest exit and try to run and get away."

She was shocked by this displacement of identity. It was something she had never thought about before.

On the way home, she reported later, she had to pull over to collect herself. It was a major insight to the change she was undergoing.

Not long ago, I was working with someone who was talking about how he had felt controlled by his mother. He was very upset, and yet he was whispering.

I pointed out the discrepancy between the angry message and the process of giving the message, that they didn't go together, and asked how it would sound if the delivery of the message was congruent with the context of the message.

He started yelling. It was much more satisfying; he felt relieved.

Interestingly, what often happens is that the counselor starts getting annoyed for the client.

If the client will not "own" a feeling, then, often, a sensitive counselor will begin to feel it. The counselor can use this information to invite the client to be more in touch with his own feelings.

Body Signals: *External movement, Internal feelings*

An endless stream of non-verbal information is available to you through your clients' involuntary movements, sounds, eye patterns, and more. Of course, you cannot respond to it all, nor would you want to. However, if you pick up a strong signal or pattern of movement that accompanies something the client is expressing, even when she is silent, you may want to include it as additional data. Here are some examples from my practice.

"I notice that while you're talking about the way your wife has responded to your telling her that you want to shave your legs, *your* leg is swinging back and forth at a rapid pace. I am wondering what your leg can tell us. What is the feeling going on in that leg?"

The client might say that he is anxious about this discussion, or wants to get it over with fast, or that he's annoyed. He is usually not conscious that some movement is happening with one part of his body until it is brought to his attention. Then it becomes a valuable clue to both client and counselor, and they can explore these feelings together.

Sometimes the counselor experiences an unusually strong empathic reaction or feels perplexed by something that's happening with the client.

If the counselor is aware, she can learn from the experience and may be able to use it productively with the client. If the counselor is not aware, then her interventions may actually hinder and confuse the client.

One way to use it productively is to say something like, "Hey, I just had quite a reaction." If you share it as your feeling and not something he did to you, you can ask your client what he is aware of, and this can lead to a productive dialogue.

Sometimes the signal appears in you rather than your client! Recently I found that while a client was talking I started getting sleepy. It was a tremendous effort to stay awake and aware.

I was actually bored, so I took the risk of saying to this person, "I'm having a terrible time staying awake, and I am wondering what it is that's going on that makes me feel like this is so boring that I can't really stay present the way I want to."

This comment led to a wonderful process in which my client came to the realization that he was not taking many risks. He kept staying with safe topics. He himself was bored with what he was saying.

He thanked me, and at the next session said, "That was really one of the most helpful interventions you made, because it helped me become aware of what I was doing, and I know you were saying it with love."

That's what the client is there for, to get feedback from you and have an honest relationship. If you say something with love and caring, you can share practically any true response, and it can be of value to the client.

Tactile Information

Using material such as blocks, clay, or crayons provides ways to generate data and supplement the usual communication patterns. Some people use little dolls or figures. I keep two teddy bears in my office, a large one and a small one. I bring them out at various times if a person needs comfort or needs to show a relationship between a parent and a child.

Sometimes it's much easier for the client to express herself when she holds those external objects. You might try to think about what kind of materials you can have around your office to help your client express herself more fully.

Role Playing

It is vital to check any of the client's polarities. This is especially important in gender work.

The client needs to explore the side with which he is less familiar, or at least create a dialogue between or among the different aspects of himself.

I have coined a new word, "polygenderism," to describe someone who recognizes that he is in a dynamic process and is not exactly the same gender all the time; he evidences various forms of gender identity that move and flow from one to the other (and all points in between.)

Sometimes part of the person really likes the whole experience of gender expression; another part is very negative and wishes it would go away.

In humanistic Gestalt therapy, one technique is to bring in empty chairs and have each chair represent a different aspect of this person. You have these parts start a dialogue and lay out the problem. You encourage the client to switch chairs each time a new part wishes to speak. Eventually, the parts will seek an integration when the client realizes that each and every part has value and can contribute to the whole.

Some clients are resistant to role playing in any form. If so, you can go to one of the other sensory routes such as drawing the parts and talking about them or experimenting with how each part moves. By watching your client's signals, you will soon be able to pick up which channel of exploration is available, or you can just ask!

***

This has been a basic introduction to the uses of sensory data and experiments. If you are interested in more information about this type of work, see some of the books listed in the Appendix by Arnold Mindell, Fritz Perls, and Janie Rhyne. Also, Lesley College in Cambridge, Massachusetts has an Expressive Therapies program, or you can investigate a supervision group with someone who has this background.

CHAPTER FOUR

GROUP WORK

It cannot be emphasized enough how important personal growth group work is with this population.

If I had to choose only one format in which transgendered people could work, it would be the group. There are four reasons for this:

1. They are with other people who are engaged in a similar process, so they don't have to explain themselves from scratch.

2. They can begin to see individual differences between themselves and others. They learn where different people are on this path, and how they feel about themselves in relation to other people's positions.

3. They can get feedback and encouragement from people like themselves, and have more than the counselor's views about how they are proceeding. They can get all kinds of ideas and suggestions from other transgendered people.

4. They are in a situation where many different kinds of themes will be explored, (not just their own experience or ideas about it), which will then provide them with a broader perspective.

I facilitated a group for "T's" for five years. When the group began, it involved simple support, and provided a place where group members could tell their stories and feel as though they weren't isolated--weren't freaks. They were also able to experiment with dressing and/or not dressing with and in front of each other, and feel safe.

Persons in the group had done all kinds of crossdressing. On one extreme was a transsexual woman who was very disinterested in clothes. She wore jeans and a sweatshirt. Another person might have arrived in a vinyl dress, a fetishistic article that's laced on the sides and reveals a good bit of the body. Somebody else might have come in a very feminine outfit with high heels, and still another might have arrived in a business suit. In a group, all of these personas get a chance to meet each other, to say how they feel in the way they are presenting themselves, and to get reactions from the people around them.

In addition to having had a female co-facilitator the last year, I invited another "born woman" to come to the group. She was the wife of one of the members. She is studying to be a counselor, and the group was part of her training. Her presence turned out to be very helpful because the other crossdressers could get a wife's viewpoint, and she could also reveal some of her deeper feelings.

Many forms of expression can occur in groups. We have done groups on how people move--what feminine movement feels like, and what masculine movement feels like. Sometimes people bring songs that have special significance for them, or pieces of music that touch them. We have also done art work. Once the group watched a couple of relevant videos and then discussed how the videos affected them. Creative approaches help group members experience their gender exploration more comprehensively.

If the group is well run and develops accordingly, it will evolve into a community. People learn to care about each other, then take that caring outside the group meetings. They may call each other during transitions, when SRS is going on, or when someone is having a hard time with work or with his wife. It becomes a real support group beyond the actual counseling. This contrasts with a traditional psychoanalytic therapy group in which members are not expected to have contact outside the group.

Another positive aspect of the group, from the business point of view, is that it is a very efficient way to manage your practice. In the same amount of time that you would use to see two or three clients, you see ten or twelve people who are each paying a group fee. It's an efficient and good use of your time and an effective way to generate additional income. Group work is a practical option for counselors who are worried about their individual private practices.

On the down side, the same thing happens in groups as occurs in private practice at a higher rate than with other types of clients. People drop out, disappear, have trouble keeping their agreements about paying on time. Even when I have made written contracts with people, some are unable to live up to them. I collect a half fee for missed sessions which are not announced in advance.

Unfortunately, the drop-outs are rarely willing to work through the reasons for, and feelings behind, their exits. There are also people who are steadfast, come to every possible meeting and are obviously committed to the process.

During the time of economic hardship, when some people lost jobs, I established a sliding scale so everyone could keep coming to the group.

It is a good idea to interview potential group members who are not personally known to you, to assess their readiness for this type of learning venue and their commitment to showing up as well as making payments on time.

Each counselor must determine what kind of agreement she wants to make with group members--and the consequences if agreements are not kept. Doing groups is not for everyone. If you are definitely a one-on-one counselor, you can send your client to a group.

PART III

RELATIONSHIPS

"Curiouser and curiouser!..."

Lewis Carroll

INTRODUCTION

Many of the problems facing gender-challenged couples have less to do with the gender issue per se and more to do with such considerations as:

- The amount and type of dysfunctionality in their families of origin
- How this affects their perceptions of each other
- Whether important information and secrets were or weren't shared
- How this relates to their decisions about telling current significant persons about their gender issue
- How capable they are of resolving unfinished situations from their past so they can work effectively with current challenges
- How effectively they communicate
- How well they can do at each being responsible for their own feelings and actions, as well as being able to state their needs and concerns clearly
- How much genuine love and support exists between them to give them the strength to work on the complex issue of gender expression

The following chapters will elaborate on each of these considerations and will also provide some guidelines for helping couples to work on the gender issue itself.

CHAPTER 1

FAMILY BACKGROUND

A big challenge for the counselor is to make sure that dysfunctionality issues are worked on and separated from the gender issues.

If either partner comes from a dysfunctional family, that is, a family in which there was, for example, an alcoholic, a drug user, an abuser (sexual or emotional), a batterer, a gambler or a neglecter, then that person is going to carry some of that baggage into the relationship with the spouse or partner.

Spouses may not be able to separate the abusive or neglectful parent from their partners, and may have fantasies about what their partner is going to do if they say or do certain things. If they believe their fantasies are facts, and don't check out the partner's true feelings, trouble may ensue.

The counselor needs to help the "T" recognize what has been carried into this relationship from the primary family, and then work with the client to separate gender issues from other issues. This can be accomplished in individual sessions with the "T".

On the wife's part, she may have all the same kind of "baggage" in her background. Suppose, for instance, she grew up in a family where she never knew how her alcoholic father was going to act when he came home (or what was going to come out of his mouth), and lived in a state of constant terror. Now she is married to a person who demonstrates these unusual "T" feelings that come and go.

99

So she feels unsafe most of the time because she doesn't know what's going to happen next. Again, she needs to finish her unfinished business from the past which caused her initial insecurity. Once she has done that, she can begin to see her spouse or partner as a separate person, and can deal with present issues, including the gender challenge, more effectively.

CHAPTER 2

THE COMMUNICATION PROCESS

Another factor in working with couples involves their communication process. How have they been communicating since they've been together? How does each of them feel about the way other problems in this partnership are addressed?

I ask them, for example, how they work on differences of opinion about the house, about money, about work, about where to go on vacation. As they describe to me how they communicate about these ordinary relationship concerns, I get a pretty good idea about where the weaknesses are, where their strengths and resources reside, and how they can use these strengths in working with the gender issues. I try to get them to tell me what they already know, and then apply it to what they need to understand in this situation.

I had one client, "Harry," who came to counseling thinking there was nothing wrong with his marriage. In fact, he was in total denial. His background included a father who drank, and yet he never really thought, "My father is an alcoholic; that's why certain things happened when I was a kid which are happening again in my marriage."

If good communication has never been modeled in the primary family, he has no idea what a good marriage or what intimacy should look like. Part of the way to learn is through the relationship with the counselor. Often this is the first time the person has ever been encouraged to talk about personal and intimate things (rather than being punished or ignored). Through

101

counseling, it slowly became apparent to Harry that he had an unsatisfying marriage based on denial of his real needs and gifts, including his gender expression. Slowly, he began to have some sense of what he wanted from a partner and what he had to offer. (He has since remarried.)

Something which can happen, and often does, is that the whole relationship gets blown out of the water with the presentation of the gender issue.

The "T" realizes, or both partners realize, that the marriage was built on false premises: they had a lot of neurotic needs; they had been leaning on each other; they had very little in common; they don't like to solve problems together, they don't really love each other.

Facing these circumstances, they may decide to end their marriage and start their separate lives somewhere else.

Making the decision to separate is difficult, especially if children are involved. At least the couple can get to the point where they are looking realistically at the relationship and deciding whether it is worth the effort to stay together (essentially to create a new relationship), or whether they would be better off going their own ways.

Sometimes, unfortunately, this decision has to be made unilaterally. One person simply does not want to stay in the relationship under certain conditions. The other partner wants the relationship to continue, but there are irreconcilable issues.

CHAPTER 3

ADDRESSING GENDER ISSUES

Crossdressers

Finally, couples need to work with the gender issues themselves. It is important to define specific problems rather than allowing the client to generalize. A new client may tell me "This gender thing is killing me. I can't do anything right. My wife just doesn't like anything I do."

I will ask, "Specifically, what doesn't she like? What gives you trouble?" We get down to details, such as her repulsion with his long fingernails, or dislike of his leg hair removal, or fear about going to a local mall where one might be recognized.

The counselor can't of be much help until specific concerns are identified.

Make sure each partner knows what issue they are dealing with, and keep the focus on that particular issue before you move to another one. Don't try to throw everything into the same pot. What you'll get is a stew.

It takes a secure, self-confident woman to be able to put up with all of the different mind-sets and feeling states of the crossdresser. She may need individual counseling and support throughout this exploration.

Sometimes it's difficult to figure out what's going to satisfy each of them without the other person having to make major lifestyle changes in order to accommodate. But with careful and specific agreements which get reviewed from time to time, it is possible to work through these challenges.

Transsexuals

The situation with transsexuals (woman-identified but born and raised as male) and their female partners is somewhat different from that of crossdressers. In some ways it's more clear-cut.

If the transsexual is definitely on the path of transition and can no longer put aside her own life for the comfort of the other person, then that fact must get communicated to the spouse or partner.

The wife may have a variety of responses, including, "I love you no matter what, and I want to stay even if you turn into a chicken. We may have to change our sex practices because I don't think I would really want to touch your breasts, but there is no question that I love you and that this has been a good partnership for us."

If sex is not an issue for either person and they have a basically good relationship, there may be no reason for them to separate (except in the eyes of the law). They can still be loving and affectionate.

But if sex is important or is an issue for either one, they may have problems (unless both are transsexual or bisexual).

Often, a wife may have strong negative reactions at first; as the process goes along, she may be able to come to terms with the partner's changing appearance, then look beyond the gender assignation to the human being.

She may think about what it means for this person to change a familiar male body to an unrecognized woman's body. She may need to ask herself what this has to do with her feelings of devotion to this person.

In the ideal situation, the partners do a lot of talking about the internal needs of the role, the cosmetic needs, the different kinds of feelings, and how transsexualism infringes on, and in some cases enhances, what they have as a couple. Often, a very different kind of relationship evolves from the one into which she originally entered. But it's clear that a real transition is taking place and a new relationship must be forged taking these changes into account.

Sometimes, the sexual orientation shifts. Once the transsexual has changed her body image to fit her inner identity, she may find herself fantasizing about male lovers, and want a partnership with a man. Even in a formerly gay relationship with a man, this may cause problems for the transsexual's partner who now faces dealing with a woman's body, and may no longer feel desire. It's complicated and must be explored slowly and sensitively by counselor and clients.

CHAPTER 4

COMING OUT OF THE CLOSET

Of all the problems that beset the transgendered person, probably one that creates the most pain has to do with relationships and how gender identity issues affect the couple. The first issue to be faced is what and how to tell his partner.

Telling the Partner

If a male-to-female crossdresser or a transsexually inclined male is in a relationship with a woman, he can experience a major struggle with regard to whether and how to tell her. What will her reactions be? What should he do about them? What are her rights and needs? What are his rights and needs?

Some people live for years with a partner without telling her about this most important part of their existence, therefore living what is, essentially, a duplicitous life.

I have met wives who, after thirty years of marriage, had only recently found out about their husband's crossdressing. The major blow to the wife was the betrayal, not the phenomenon of the crossdressing itself. The fact that this person, about whom they thought they knew everything and with whom they thought they had an intimate relationship, had not told them that a major portion of his psyche was preoccupied with *femme* matters is a great shock.

Wives discover their husband's "T"ism in a variety of ways.

The husband seeks counseling, thinking that he is only going to be talking about himself and his own situation, and the counselor says, "How does your wife figure in all this?" We have long talks about why keeping the woman in his life uninformed doesn't work in the long run, unless he wants an extremely superficial marriage.

The next step to be addressed is the matter of telling her: how to tell her, what to tell her, how to deal with her reactions.

Sometimes the man desperately wants the woman to find out, but is afraid of telling her. So he "unconsciously" leaves some evidence around which she then finds. She may discover a bag of clothes in the car, or a false fingernail on the sink, or something stashed away in the attic that doesn't belong there. So she confronts him with it. At first she may think that she has found evidence of an affair, but then the story comes out.

What happens when the partner of a transgendered person finds out about the transgendered behavior?

Betrayal is the major concern, especially if the couple has been together for some time. If he lied about something so important, what else is he covering up? He tries to reassure her that he hasn't kept anything else from her (except, of course, all of his intense feelings). But it takes a long time for the trust to be built up again.

The revelation often takes place because the man has a crisis of conscience and realizes that, for his own peace of mind, he must talk to her. He can't hide the truth any longer.

Early in the relationship, he may have made some attempt to talk about crossdressing, hinted around, or even made an outright confession. Then both of them go into denial and live as though neither one of them knows, until some later incident makes her recognize that the behavior has not disappeared.

She may, in the initial confession, threaten him and say, "If you ever do this again, I am going to leave you." So he goes underground; he doesn't talk about it. Then, years later, the subject comes up again, and now has to be dealt with.

When he does decide to speak to her about this important aspect of his being, no matter when it occurs in their relationship, hopefully it will be in circumstances where neither of them will be interrupted, where they have privacy and where each person will be able to express feelings, ask questions and communicate as fully as possible about it. Often, even though it is difficult and painful to talk about, both people experience some relief that the truth is finally out where they can deal with it one way or the other.

The wife must be allowed and encouraged to give free rein to all of her feelings. The more she can do this with impunity, the more possibility there is for the couple to make a good adjustment later on. Be suspicious of a wife who appears to be totally supportive and delighted with the whole thing immediately. Often, when the novelty wears off, these women's feelings change and they become angry or withdrawn. Encourage her to get to her questions and possible problems with her husband's gender expression early on.

Telling the Children

Issues also arise with regard to telling the children, especially older children.

The "T" may think this is a big secret that the kids know nothing about, but younger people are often very sensitive to nonverbal behavior, language, and all kinds of signs and clues regarding gender. They might find something in the laundry, or see something they don't recognize as their mother's, or notice that an item of women's clothing is a different size. Many of them who were told about a parent's crossdressing turn out not be surprised at all. Much to the parents' amazement, the children sensed something already.

The "T" needs to ask himself, "Would I rather have the children find out from me or from somebody else who may be out to do me harm? Would I prefer to have their mother tell them, or me, or both of us together? Do I want to wait until they ask questions? Do I want to sound them out by seeing how they react to certain movies like *Tootsie*, and gauge how open or anxious their reactions are?"

Some people tell their children and others do not. There are many different reasons for either decision.

As a counselor, I believe my job is to help the couple explore their feelings about the possible choices: why they would want to tell or not want to tell, how each partner feels about the possibilities, what would be the need to know and/or the need to tell? Gradually, as a couple discusses these questions, the decision becomes clearer.

In my first year at Fantasia Fair working with the wives' group, I found that none of the couples had told their kids. Now all of them have. Often their predictions about how each child would respond were incorrect; there is often no way of telling in advance how each child will react.

The couple may have differences about whether to tell the children. They may have to make a decision that, for now, as long as one partner feels severely uncomfortable, the children won't be told. However, the uncomfortable partner will be encouraged to keep exploring his or her fear. In other words, that person has to take responsibility for these feelings. It's not OK to say to the partner "Just don't tell, and that's it" because that's a parental way of relating. It's like saying to your child, "Because I said so, that's why you have to do it."

Adults need to share feelings and reasons with each other in an open dialogue. Sometimes a couple reaches an agreement, and then a month later the issue is brought up again. At that time, we discuss each person's feelings about the issue.

In general, children have a much less difficult time dealing with knowing about the transgendered behavior than do adults.

If the father talks to them when they are still quite young, it's usually no problem at all for them because they don't categorize in the same way adults do. They take each person as he or she comes, as long as they feel cared about.

On the other hand, the "T" needs to be counseled about how this information might affect the child's life outside the home. How might it affect their school life? What if their friends ask questions? How can a transsexual make it safe and comfortable for the child to have such a different kind of parent? What happens when the parent visits the school?

One of my transgendered clients does have this very situation. Her child is now calling her father by her official femme name rather than using Daddy as she did before. The basic relationship, however, has not changed. The father has spoken to the child's teachers and counselor and has explained his (her) transition. She answers any questions they might have. She can now come and go at school with the assurance that support exists within the school system and that children with questions will get appropriate information.

For crossdressers, whether or not to tell the children is based primarily on the need to know . Certainly, if the kids are living at home and the crossdresser wants to use his home in which to dress, he may need to tell them.

If his children are teenagers, he may need to negotiate with them. He might say, "Before you come home, call me because I'll be dressing " or "I'm going to be using some time this weekend to dress so make your plans accordingly. If it doesn't bother you, it's fine for you to be around. I'll just be working in the kitchen . If it does bother you, you need to make other plans."

If the crossdresser dresses in places other than the home, or if he dresses only in the bedroom and the door has a lock on it, there may be no need for the kids to know. A lot of private things go on in the bedroom, and this can just be one of them; the kids don't need explanations.

However, if children ask direct questions, they should be answered honestly and briefly. The "T" can then see if that answer satisfies the child or if the child wants more information. Take the lead from the child, rather than inundating her with information for which she may not be ready .

Who the children are, how old they are and what stage of development they are in, what they do with new information, how they have been brought up, the values of the family about sharing intimate information, what else has been shared and dealt with well in this family--all of this must be taken into account by you, the counselor, as you attempt to help these people with their decision about telling their children.

Telling Parents

Often, "T's" think of their parents as totally unaccepting, or have had a falling out with them. It is very important for these parents to know what is going on, especially the parents of transsexuals. Parents of crossdressers may not have a need to know. But if a transsexual is going to have a continuing relationship with his parents, it is imperative that they be given a full explanation. After all, the "T" is going to look very different!

If a transsexual person is overwhelmed by the prospect of talking to her parents, I suggest bringing parents along to our counseling session. Then I help the "T" and the parents to hear each other, to practice good communication, and to air their feelings. The counselor can educate the parents in a way that the "T" cannot, can give them objective information, encourage their questions.

It is a very different effect for the "T" to tell the parent, "I'm really a girl," than for a professional person to explain. I point out that I have been dealing with this phenomenon for a long time, then describe what can and cannot be changed. I tell them what I hope will happen in their relationship in order for the "T" to have the best possible experience. I express my concern about the parent's feelings, then encourage the adult child, the "T," to listen to the parent's worries, concerns, incredulity and whatever other reactions are expressed. It is important that the "T" not dismiss the feelings as being invalid, but really listen to each one and deal honestly with them. The parents, too, need to listen respectfully to what their child is telling them.

Often parents express the fear that their child is going to get attacked or murdered or hurt in some way. Although there is not a huge chance of physical danger there is probably more of a chance that a "T," or a woman, could be attacked than a non-trans-gendered man. On the other hand, violence in our culture is a prominent problem and can occur against anyone at any time.

So I first try to put things into perspective. Then I ask the "T" to discuss her own safety concerns and tell the parents what she/he is doing about them. Generally, the parents are not as anxious once they know that their "T" child is learning to handle difficult situations and knows how to protect herself.

Telling Other Family

Suppose the man tells his wife that he wants to inform his family of origin about his crossdressing. He knows he will feel relieved; he doesn't want to live this lie anymore. Then she says, "Nothing doing. This has to stay between us. I don't want anyone else to know."

The counselor can ask each of them to go into their reasons for wanting to tell or not tell, and can explore with them what is negotiable.

The wife might agree, for instance, that he can tell his sister if he first gets an agreement from her that she is willing to keep confidential whatever he shares with her. Has he been able to trust her in this way in the past? If the wife knows that the sister is not a gossip, maybe then she will agree and the "T" will have some relief.

Sometimes the wife tells the secret to all family members without his permission. It is often an act of revenge for her hurt feelings of having felt betrayed by him (not telling her or even just being the way he is).

Then you, as their counselor, need to help them face their anger toward each other as one issue, and how the "T" now wants to handle this new situation with their relatives as another. Sometimes the "T" wants to talk with them face to face. Sometimes he wants to see if they will approach him. In either case, he needs to make a conscious decision.

A danger exists that if the marriage is very shaky, this act on the wife's part may cause irreparable damage. On the other hand, it is sometimes a relief to the "T" that now he doesn't have to hide this information from his relatives any longer. However, if the wife has revealed his secret in a spirit of vengeance, it can create a major issue between them, and the relatives may have erroneous ideas and information which he may want to correct.

You can help by making sure all feelings get expressed responsibly in the safety of your office. and that any mutual problem solving leads to clear agreements about how to proceed and who is responsible for what part of the process.

Telling Friends

If the man is getting more and more uncomfortable about having to keep his crossdressing from his close friends, he may have to force the issue with his partner and say, "Look, I really need to do this. I understand that you are very uncomfortable about it, but I can no longer be responsible for your uncomfortable feelings. If you threaten to leave me, then I'm not in the marriage that I thought I was in. I need you to support my well-being. I can accommodate to you while you work through your feelings, but I may not be willing to be on hold indefinitely."

Sometimes the wife wants to tell *her* friends about her husband's crossdressing. Yet he may be a private, secretive person who doesn't want his "T" activities spread around.

The question is, whose secret is it to tell, and under what conditions? Assuming the couple is communicating well, they can decide who *needs* to know and what is each partner's *need* to tell or not tell. Of course, if the husband's appearance is going to change radically, anyone actively in their lives will need an explanation.

Telling an Employer

For a crossdressser, there is really no need to tell anyone in his place of employment about his crossdressing. For a transsexual, it's a different matter entirely.

115

As a person goes through transition, her appearance begins to change. At some point before the change becomes too radical, it is a good idea to support your client in speaking to her boss or a person in the employee assistance program (if it is available) or human resources department.

Since it is unlikely that the people at work will know much about transsexualism, it is important to bring information and resources so that they can educate themselves and understand the rights of your client. Which bathroom to use can become a major issue unless employers and fellow workers understand that, once your client has legally changed her identity, whether she has had surgery or not, she has the rights of that gender.

Sometimes, I have written a letter to the employer for the client to use in support of the changes and reorientation which must take place. In the best situations, the employer fully supports the transition and informs the staff, encouraging them to speak directly to the transsexual about their concerns or questions and, also, to be supportive.

Counseling about this disclosure in the work setting needs to be approached on a case by case basis. It does need to be addressed. Exactly how it gets handled depends on the culture of the business, how conservative, formal, visible, open it is. It depends on how good the relationships are between your client and her colleagues, how well she is doing her job and a host of other factors.

You can work with your client to help her be in the strongest possible position at her workplace prior to the disclosure. You can help her work through her fears, encourage her to rehearse different ways of responding to various reactions she imagines from others, help her strengthen her resolve to be who she truly is at work and elsewhere. You can offer your support by being willing to speak to persons in key positions about any of their concerns or questions.

Finally, you can help her partner and other family members to be encouraging and supportive as she goes through this important step.

My Bias to Tell

My own personal bias is that if there is to be true intimacy among members of a family, important secrets should be shared. Usually, less harm can occur if an issue is out in the open where it can be dealt with by all affected persons. I tell this to clients while defending their right to make their own decisions.

If it's a close-knit family, a crossdresser wants the other family members to know about this significant experience in his life. There is a large part of him that the kids may not know about and may be interested in, and soon.

However, people have the right to do what they want to about telling. You have to assess the client's value system and his personality. As they work along in counseling, some people become more and more distressed at having to keep any important secret. It weighs on their soul, and they suffer as much from that as from any aspect of the gender challenge.

Others have been conditioned to compartmentalizing, keeping information separate in different parts of their life. Because this system has worked for a long time, they feel it will continue to work.

But people and life circumstances change; the person starts developing differently; counseling may have a big effect on the person's value system and what he feels. What once was perfectly acceptable as a way of handling the situation may become completely out of the question after a while as a normal part of the maturing process.

Why is there any secrecy? Usually because there is some shame-based feeling or some anxiety, some fear, some guilt attached to the transgender behavior or wishes. One may have a strong need to control, out of a tremendous fear of being out of control.

Once these issues have been worked through, there is not too much more reason for secret keeping--from kids, from parents, from anyone close.

It is equally important for you, the counselor, to face any issues you have about secrecy in your life. You could experience extreme psychic discomfort and, therefore, be less than effective in working with your client on this issue if you have not worked out this issue for yourself. If this is a conflict, get some supervision or talk it over with a colleague.

CHAPTER 5

SEXUAL MYTHOLOGY

Another big issue is that a wife's sexual mythology about her husband is disturbed when he admits that he wants to wear women's clothes, that he gets sexual and erotic satisfaction from wearing them.

The man to whom she was initially sexually attracted and who matches her fantasies of who attracts her, turns out to be a different kind of man from the one now presenting himself to her.

Some crossdressers want to wear an article of women's clothing to bed or to include crossdressing in their sex life; others want to keep it completely separate. The latter does not pose much of a problem since he, himself, has strongly identified with his male role as a sex partner. If the wife keeps imagining the husband dressed when he is not, that becomes a problem of her own making. You can help her separate her fantasy from the reality. If he *does* express some interest in dressing in the bedroom, she now may face a real struggle if she is strongly heterosexual. She is not interested in making love with a feminized man.

He, in the meantime, may fantasize when they are together sexually that he is in the femme role. This causes her to worry that when he is with her sexually he is much more concerned about his femme experience than he is about making love to her. A rivalry and competition develops, somewhat as though he had a mistress. She wants to know how she compares with this woman he has created, with whom he seems to be completely enamored. What does it mean to him to have sex with her?

If she is really a heterosexually-driven woman who is attracted to his masculinity, and he is interested in having femme ideation and femme fantasy, the relationship is at an impasse, no matter how much they love each other.

If the two people are mature enough, sometimes they resolve the problem by finding ways to be with each other that are somewhat satisfying; but it is never truly a passionate match.

You cannot tell the woman, "Well, just change your idea of what's desirable." Our sexual desires are set very early in our lives. They are some of the strongest conditioning we have, and it is difficult, often impossible, to change them.

During the consciousness-raising time of the women's movement, many heterosexual women did decide that their emotional experiences with women were so satisfying that they reconditioned themselves to be with women sexually. But many of them, if the truth be told, were still more erotically aroused by being with men. Some discovered that they were, indeed, bisexual. In a "T's" relationship with a partner, the bisexual woman can often be responsive to him in ways that the strongly heterosexual woman finds difficult.

Older, committed couples are often able to make accommodations because their sex drive is not as strong as it was when they were in their twenties and thirties. They can still be physically affectionate, still have some kind of sex. Perhaps she can allow the man to fantasize whatever he wants, as long as he doesn't talk about it and isn't overt about it so that she can have her own fantasies. Sometimes the sexual part of their relationship simply evaporates. If sex was never very important and if it has become less important at this point in their marriage, then doing without it may not be disturbing. But if the couple is relatively young, with a high sex drive, making adjustments is quite a challenge.

CHAPTER 6

RIGHTS AND RESPONSIBILITIES OF EACH PARTNER

When I speak to wives, I make the point that the "T" is not the only person with rights, needs, and concerns in that relationship. The wife is allowed to have concerns, to set limits, to have boundaries, and to say what she can and can't handle, just as he is able to do those things. The woman needs to stand up for her own needs and rights in a marriage.

Many of the older couples with whom I have dealt come from the 1940's and 1950's form of marriage in which the man is in charge and the "little woman" supports him and helps him meet his needs; her responsibility has been simply taking care of him and the children.

The concept of marriage has changed since the women's movement. In a modern marriage, the partners need to be able to deal with each other as equals and see each other's needs as equally important. This can create some tension in a gender-challenged couple.

Women, especially, need to be gently confronted on taking their own needs seriously and being able to express their fears, so that they can figure out how they want to deal with this issue. They need to identify what seems impossible for them to handle right now.

They need time to learn to keep track of the way they are changing and growing, and to better understand their own secret desires, fantasies, and wishes.

CHAPTER 7

RISK TAKING

Other problems have to do with different levels of comfort with risk taking.

The man, for instance, may want to try some new "feminization"--shaving legs, growing nails, or piercing ears--before the woman is ready to accept or deal with those changes. If he goes ahead impulsively and acts on his feelings without consulting her, it's another betrayal.

She wants to know, "Why didn't you talk with me about this? Why didn't you tell me?"

His response is usually, "I was afraid you would say no. Then I would feel guilty." Of course, he ends up feeling guilty anyway.

One of your jobs as their counselor is to help these two people to be willing to take the risks involved in honest communicating. They need to get to a point where they can talk about anything, where they don't deny or condemn each other's feelings. If they decide they are in the relationship for the long haul and don't want to break their commitment to each other, they reach the best compromise they can on what appear to be irreconcilable differences.

CHAPTER 8

GUIDELINES FOR COUPLES

When I am working with a couple on improving their communication skills, I am teaching them to be totally present for each other without interruptions and with an attitude of respect.

I teach them active listening. They learn to hear their own and each other's apparent contradictions or unresolved problems, They feed back what they are hearing from their partners before responding, and then go on to discuss what kind of process they can use to become allies so that they can get through some of these problems and, together, produce solutions. I often guide them into making written agreements that can be reviewed later.

You can suggest that they set aside time on a regular basis to do this exercise or something similar:

Ten Steps to Working it Out
1. Make uninterrupted time for each other.
2. Sit facing each other, making eye contact.
3. Take turns speaking of your own feelings about the gender issue: your fears, curiosity, resentments, excitement.
4. Before you respond to what your partner has expressed, repeat back what you understand until he or she is satisfied and feels understood.
5. Make a list of apparent contradictions or unresolved problems.
6. Take each item on the list in turn and, as allies, try to find a solution which both of you can live with.

Include what you, yourself, can do to help bring about a good solution.

7. Write down each agreement and establish a time for evaluating how it is or isn't being carried out, as well as when it will be up for review.
8. Plan for expanding your knowledge base through reading and meeting others who have dealt with similar issues.
9. Plan pleasurable times together outside of gender activities.
10. At the end of each communication session, look at your partner and find a way to express affection.

Example of a Positive Interaction

Active listening is one of the most useful tools for you to coach your couples to include in their communication.

Here's a sample dialogue:

She: "I feel sexually turned off by your shaved legs and long fingernails. I don't want to be touched by you under those conditions."

He (using active listening): "When you see or feel my nails or shaved legs, it's a turn-off and you don't want to have sex with me."

She: "That's right."

He: "So the problem is, how can we have a satisfactory sex life if I want to keep my legs shaved and my nails on the long side?"

She: "We probably need to talk more about what turns each of us on and how or whether we can meet those conditions for each other."

He: "Here's one thing I could do. Instead of shaving all the time, I could shave for special events where I want to wear dresses in public and look good. That's maybe four or five times a year. The rest of the time I could let the hair on my legs grow back."

She: "That means there has to be enough time between any two of these events. I guess I could make an exception about shaving every once in a while if it were really inconvenient for you, but I might not be that turned on. I really can't stand the fingernails, though."

He: "If you feel that strongly about fingernails, I can keep my own nails trimmed and wear false nails for special events. If I have a very strong urge to have my own nails longer every once in a while, I could discuss it with you and maybe we could plan it into the schedule."

She: "That would be O.K. with me, provided that during that time you don't expect me to be sexually responsive. You know, what really turns me on is your man-ness, your being assertive during lovemaking, having your male sex characteristics intact, treating me as desirable and the object of your romantic interest. It's hard to do that when I think you really want to *be* me rather than make love to me."

He: "I understand that. Sometimes it is a conflict for me, but I think that if I have enough space to express the feminine side of me in other parts of my life, I can thoroughly enjoy being your husband in the bedroom ." (A male who is transsexually inclined toward womanhood might say, "Most of the time I would like to give what you need in that respect; however, some of the time I would like you to make love to me. There is an aspect of me that needs to feel wanted and cherished just like you do.")

The last consideration could also be true for a crossdressed male, with a strong male identity, but is probably not as much of an issue. An extremely transsexually-inclined male who feels she is a woman and headed for transition, might need to have long and serious talks with his/her wife about the end of their marriage as they have known it. They have to agree to live in a new kind of relationship or to part ways.

After completing an exchange on one issue, the couple may go back to the first step with other concerns. The basic idea is that, before a response is given, each person makes sure that they have heard the other to that person's satisfaction.

Guidelines for Spouses of Crossdressers

These guidelines can be given to the partners when she comes to see you or, if not, her husband can offer them to her near the beginning of his counseling.

- If either person comes from a dysfunctional family (alcohol, any sort of abuse or neglect), the gender issue will stimulate old, unconscious angers and fears that must get dealt with in order for the current relationship to work.

- Crossdressing behavior is not the reason for a bad marriage; poor communication is.

- It is nobody's fault.

- It is unknown at this time how and why the behavior exists. The feeling is not chosen; it is discovered.

- Crossdressing does not have to be addictive if well managed.

- Often, the less accepting the wife, the more compulsive the crossdresser feels.

- In relationships that work best, each person takes responsibility for any issue that affects either one strongly, and the couple communicates fully about it without blame.

- There is no known "cure" for the behavior, although the less stress and more love there is in a crossdresser's life, usually the less compulsion there is to dress and the less important it becomes to either one.

- Other issues that exist in the relationship, such as finances, child rearing, spending quality time together, etc., need to be dealt with separately from the dressing issue. If everything is blamed on the dressing, nothing will get solved.

- Any partner of a crossdresser who sincerely cannot feel love, compassion, or attraction to her partner has two choices:

  1. to work on herself and her own fears, resentment, feelings of inadequacy, and rigid beliefs

     or

  2. to decide she doesn't have enough real caring for her partner to put in the work involved, and needs to start a new life elsewhere.

The choice she doesn't have is to change her partner to meet her expectations. Paradoxically, as soon as each partner decides to take responsibility for him or herself and his/her own feelings and problems, the other person and the relationship can change for the better.

- The partner of a crossdresser has the right to set certain limits and make certain requests to get her own needs met, just as her partner does. If true caring exists in the relationship, each will come part way to meet the other's needs, or respect the other's limits without trying to control the other's behavior.

A Final Word

I have seen couples who thought they wouldn't be able to sustain their relationship and who surprised themselves and me by creating a stronger bond than they had before, Others, who seemed to be doing well with these issues have sometimes moved to a place where it became apparent that one or the other or both were unwilling to continue.

This issue has a way of profoundly stirring up the unconscious. It is important for the counselor to allow a lot of room for this complex process to unfold. It is a great opportunity for us as counselors, and for the partners, to make many discoveries, to find out all sorts of things about ourselves about which we were not formerly aware. Beware of deciding how it will come out. Just support each person and the couple in doing what feels right for them.

Occasionally, the problems and frustrations of the couple may be aimed toward you. Hopefully, they will stay around to work it out and find out about the real source of their anger and unhappiness. Sometimes there may be destructive acting out or disappearing. Do what you can to encourage them to work it through. If they (or either one) refuse and insist on blaming you for whatever pains them, do not blame yourself or assume that you were a failure. It is important that you work out whatever feelings you do have with a trusted colleague or supervisor so they do not affect other couple work you are doing.

If the partners have been together for awhile, have love and respect for themselves and each other, and have a good track record of being effective, collaborative problem solvers, if they are both strongly committed to making it work, and you can help them learn and can coach them in the skills they lack, there is a good chance their relationship will prevail and flourish.

Of course, if you find that you, yourself, have prejudices or strong negative reactions you just can't seem to relinquish, then working with gender-challenged couples is probably not a good idea for the time being.

However, if you are fascinated and thrilled by the possibilities of human potential in coupledom, and can truly be supportive of each person's process of exploration, no matter where it leads the couple, or what you may discover about yourself, there is probably no more exciting or interesting sort of counseling with which to be involved.

PART IV

PERSONAL HISTORIES

He thought he saw a Buffalo
Upon the chimneypiece.
He looked again and found it was
His sister's husband's niece!

Lewis Carroll

133

INTRODUCTION

In this section, I would like to introduce you to some human beings with whom I have had the privilege to work. They will tell you some of their stories in response to these questions:

- What would you like counselors to know about your journey before and during counseling?
- What impact did the counseling experience have on you and your life?
- What would you like to tell future gender counselors that you think is important for them to know?

Rather than expecting a literal response to each question, I asked my contributors to write or say whatever came to mind in mulling over these questions.

I have not edited these contributions, so the word "therapy" is used most frequently to describe what I have been calling the counseling process.

When clients wanted me to use their real names, I did. When they preferred not to be identified, I used pseudonyms or role designations like "husband."

The stories speak for themselves. I will not comment on them but will suggest that if you read them carefully, you will learn a lot about the issues, the pain, the vulnerabilities, the strengths and the joys which go along with a person's attempt to become conscious about gender identity and life choices.

135

A Crossdressing Husband and His Wife

Husband

I probably began physically crossdressing some time in junior high, when I was around 13 or 14. I was able to live with it, but I knew inside me it was wrong, that I shouldn't be doing it. I remember thinking periodically that I really should see somebody, but even the thought of talking to a psychiatrist was just not a possibility.

While I was married to my first wife I went through a crisis, and saw a psychiatrist a few times. It was clear to me that he thought crossdressing was abnormal, and eventually these desires should go away. There was no mention that it might be all right to do. My sense was that this is wrong, I'm wrong, I shouldn't be doing crossdressing.

It took me about ten years before I went for professional help again. I had been dressing in a closeted kind of action. It was always myself, closeted, sexual arousal; the ending was always a sexual release.

One night I sat there--I drank at least a six-pack and a half or so--drunker than hell, but not unusual for me--and I said to myself, "I don't want to go on living this way the rest of my life. I've got to see somebody." I picked up a *Tapestry* magazine and found Niela Miller's ad.

A year earlier I had actually called Niela a couple of times; but I kept getting her answering machine, so I never left a message. Now I called and got her. We talked briefly and made an appointment for the next day. I used a fake name, and then after the first appointment I gave her my real name.

Next to jumping out of an airplane, keeping the appointment was the most frightening thing I have ever done. I drove a very long roundabout route, making sure nobody was following me. I just knew everybody who passed me and looked at me understood what I was doing, where I was going, and why I was doing it. It was the most vivid feeling.

I parked quite far away from Niela's condo and sat in my car to be sure nobody had been following me. As I walked the route to her house I stopped several times to make sure I was alone.

Her approach, at first, was to help me believe crossdressing was OK, that there were other crossdressers.

But there was so much more that was not working in my life than the crossdressing. The progress actually was quite slow at first. I started feeling better and better about dressing, although I'm still working on that. But because the rest of my life didn't change, I got more and more frustrated. It got harder and harder to deal with my life, because my wife, at the time, was not at all accepting. Things actually got more confused, I think, rather than more clear.

I made a couple of close friends, through Niela's introductions. I think working with Niela gave me the confidence, or just the insight, to feel that it's OK to have friends who crossdress.

I remember vividly one time when she sort of cradled my head in her hands; it was a sense of nurturing that I had never felt before, and was an extremely emotional time. It lasted just a minute or two but it was certainly a breakthrough with what I have worked on subsequently about being nourished and nurtured.

Niela's primary thrust initially was to get me to accept my crossdressing. I remember her saying many times there was so much more for me to work on. And I kept thinking no: once I get OK with being able to dress, then I don't have much more to do. However, it was clear there was a lot more work to be done.

Eventually I made a deal with my wife, now ex-wife, that Tuesday nights could be mine. I went to a crossdressers' club usually on Tuesday nights. I got less guilty about my crossdressing, but I think I got more frustrated because I still had the old constraints on me. I didn't have to feel crappy about myself, but I still had a family, and a wife who thought I was disgusting.

Every Tuesday night when I had to change to come home, I felt a deep sense of loss and of sadness. At times it was almost painful. Ironically, as I started feeling better about my crossdressing, I had deeper pain associated with leaving it behind.

After I met my present wife, but before I separated from my ex-wife, I saw another therapist, who specialized in marriage counseling. My ex-wife and I went infrequently. Although it was helpful, it didn't save the marriage.

For the past three or four years I have been seeing another counselor. While crossdressing comes up frequently because it's an issue in my life, we don't work on the crossdressing. We work on other life issues.

My counselor is totally accepting of the crossdressing. In fact, once as we were discussing some stresses in my original family, he said, "What a wonderful escape. A lot of people are into drugs, alcohol, or whatever, and look what you chose." So he doesn't have any problem with crossdressing, and we don't really work on it specifically.

If I knew earlier what I know now, I certainly would have sought help earlier. Part of my struggle has been, I think, that I have extremes in my personality.

I like to think that I am very masculine and I do some macho kind of things, and that macho part of me has had trouble accepting the other part of me. If I could have accepted those sides of me much earlier, life would have been a whole lot more pleasant for many more years.

In the past, I have said that crossdressing is a part of me, that being in the Navy Reserve is part of me. Now I'm throwing out the word "part," and just saying that crossdressing is me and being in the Navy is me. When it's only a part, then the other part has to speak up too.

But all of it is me and there are no individual parts; it's all me.

Wife

I knew that Niela had been involved in counseling the transgendered for a number of years. The day that I met "D," our women's group had spent the afternoon talking about the topic of

crossdressing, looking at pictures taken by Mariette Pathy Allen*
and reading *Tapestry* magazine. Then "D" and three others
walked in. I got to spend an evening talking about it, learning
about it, and meeting the crossdressers (actually one or two were
transsexuals). One is now a post-operative transsexual.

When I met him, "D" was still married to his former wife.

Probably far greater an issue than the crossdressing was the
fact that he was still married and living with another woman; that
went on for seven months. Although we saw Niela together just
before "D" left his former wife, that session really had little or
nothing to do with the crossdressing.

Crossdressing for me was just never an issue. It was
something unusual and out of the ordinary and very new to me,
but the fact that I met my husband when he was crossdressed
meant that I had heard and seen his biggest secret from the very
first moment that we met. So I was anxious to find out more about
it. It soon became clear to me that one of the things I could do in
this relationship was to encourage "D" to express himself in this
way. The level of shame and disgrace and (everything else he felt
that was negative about it) just didn't exist for me.

Perhaps the fact that crossdressing wasn't an issue for me
has to do with things that have happened in my own life. I've had
two siblings commit suicide. As I have said many, many times to
'D,' "Look what happened in my family when people had
problems! You want to put on a dress, put on a dress."

I'm just a pretty open person--I'm open to new experiences
and trying new things. I knew when I saw this person that it was

*Transformations by Mariette Pathy Allen, E. P. Dutton, Inc., 1989

141

somebody I wanted to get close to and be with, and it didn't matter that he wears dresses.

I would say the issues with his former wife and the six children that we jointly share have been far more troublesome and challenging than any of the crossdressing stuff. Some issues have come up from time to time that are directly related to crossdressing, but I don't see they are any greater than anything else we deal with in our marriage.

Speaking from a wife's point of view, I would say that the therapy that "D" had leading up to the time at which he and I met has helped him tremendously. My interpretation is that the therapy was opening him up to the possibility that crossdressing might be something acceptable in himself, and that he might even be open to all kinds of new experiences and possibilities in his life.

We first met at Niela's and then had no idea when we would see each other again. A month later we both showed up for a group Niela ran called "The Living Soul." It met once a month for five months.

Prior to that time in his life, "D" would never have considered a group like this one. I think the process of his year and a half in therapy with Niela had opened him up to all kinds of new possibilities. Also, coming to her house crossdressed that day we met was something I don't think "D" would have considered doing in his life prior to that time.

So from what he has told me and what I have observed over the years, one of the most important aspects of his therapy was his ability to open to new possibilities, new discoveries, and new ways of being. I think also the self-esteem factor is of paramount importance--his beginning to learn to accept and maybe even like those parts of himself he had been so ashamed of prior to that time.

In the past few years, I've met a number of crossdressers and transsexuals who haven't done any personal growth work in terms of therapy. I cannot imagine anyone living a life without this kind of introspection, regardless of what he or she may do in their spare time. Especially for a person who does this sort of thing--it seems as though it would be most exciting to work with a therapist and try to discover where all these feelings came from. I have experienced some frustration in talking to some of the transgendered people who haven't done any therapy, because it's just so far from my belief in what we humans can do when we get help from someone who can enable us to open ourselves up and look inside.

I know a woman who's been involved with a couple of crossdressers. What became apparent very quickly in talking with her is that her involvement with a crossdresser is only a tiny aspect of her life. Her issues are way, way bigger than the fact that she may be attracted to men who wear dresses.

I think that's a very important concept for a crossdresser or a transsexual to discover in therapy, that they may have spent most or all of their lives thinking that there's just nothing in their life except this one big, enormous issue. When they get into therapy and start meeting other people and talking about the situation, they tend to discover there's just so much other stuff involved in being human and living a life. It's a fascinating process.

I just think everyone ought to examine himself/herself, whether it's men who wear dresses or whatever it is. That's one of the joys of being human as far as I'm concerned.

It's just digging into who we really are.

JAMIE: Transsexual Woman Born Biological Male

By the fall of 1988, I had already been to two therapists. The first person I went to, in early 1988, told me in our second meeting that I was hiding something. I got scared and never went back to him.

By the summer, I was ready to try therapy again.

Ostensibly, I went to discuss my relationship with the woman with whom I was having an affair. After a few weeks, I told my second therapist about my gender conflict, and he ignored it. We never discussed the gender issue in depth, concentrating instead on my relationships with the women in my life. It became obvious to me that we were not talking about the most important woman--the one who lived inside of me.

After about four months I formally ended the therapy, having *de facto* stopped by missing most of my appointments for the last month and a half. Two attempts at therapy, two failures.

I was at the lowest ebb of my life, and entertained thoughts of suicide. I was 35 years old and knew, KNEW, that if I didn't start talking about my gender conflict I would not live to my 40th birthday. In desperation I telephoned the International Foundation for Gender Education (IFGE), an information clearing house in Waltham, Mass., hoping they could recommend a therapist for me. I was told to try Niela Miller, a woman with many years of experience counseling the gender-conflicted.

During our initial contact over the telephone, I fought back tears as I described my "sexual problem." Niela calmly responded by telling me that I didn't have a sexual problem--she said I had an identity crisis. My tears of pain turned to tears of joy--I had found someone who understood. That was November, 1988.

I had been in therapy with Niela for a number of months before I openly admitted to her that I was transsexual, although she had already come to that conclusion.

Despite plenty of encouragement, I steadfastly refused to display my feminine side. Finally, after one year, Niela gave me an ultimatum: bring some women's clothes and be prepared to wear them during our next session or don't bother to come back. The next time I saw Niela, I was wearing a blue sweater and a blue plaid skirt.

A significant portion of my first year's therapy with Niela was devoted to analyzing my dreams. I hesitate to use the word "analyze" because I didn't then, and still don't now, believe that dreams can be literally interpreted. However, we were examining the dreams not for their content but for their emotional power.

It turned out to be time well spent. Initially my dreams indicated a sense of desperation. Over time, though, Niela said my dreams started to show a sense of hope. What they said to me was that I was on the right path.

As most male-to-female transsexuals, I was fairly eager to start taking female hormones. Niela didn't think I was ready. Actually, I didn't think I was ready either, so I started something else: electrolysis. Personally, I think all therapists should steer their patients into electrolysis before hormones. Almost every person I know who started hormones first is still undergoing electrolysis years beyond the time in which it should have been completed. When I ask why it's taking so long, they usually tell me it's because they can't take the pain for more than an hour (or less) a week. If you predicate hormones on the completion of electrolysis, then beard removal becomes a priority and actually gets completed within a reasonable period of time. No one should have to shave while in the hospital for sex reassignment surgery.

Niela made it clear to me from the beginning that the purpose of the therapy was not to prepare me for gender reassignment but to make my life work for me. It would be up to me to decide whether changing my gender would make me happier. She would support whatever decision I made, as long as it was my decision, freely arrived at after serious contemplation.

To that end, though, she did suggest some experiences that would help me decide. Electrolysis was one. Fantasia Fair was another. Fantasia Fair is a week-long convention of crossdressers and transsexuals, held annually in Provincetown, Massachusetts. Fantasia Fair afforded me the opportunity to live as a woman 24 hours a day, in a safe and supportive environment. I was able to meet other transsexuals and learn about their experiences, both good and bad. Most important of all, it was a laboratory in which I was able to examine my own heart and emotions and ask myself, "Do I really want to be a woman?" The answer was yes.

Even though it was obvious that I was much happier as a woman than as a man, I resisted the transition. I just couldn't seem to act on my own behalf, while at the same time I complained about my miserable life. Niela described me as a "professional victim."

One day she asked me a question: what did I get out of being unhappy? I must get something from it, otherwise I would change. So what pleasure did I receive from being unhappy? In six years of therapy, this was the single most important thing that Niela ever said to me. If I was miserable, why didn't I change? The answer was nothing less than the key to the rest of my life.

Misery was the only existence I knew. Being a "professional victim" was my self-identity--if you took that away from me, I had nothing. The absence of sorrow is not the same thing as joy--without sorrow, I felt empty inside. I realized that I was <u>choosing</u> to stay unhappy because it was the only life I knew.

But, I asked myself, if I was choosing to be a professional victim, couldn't I also choose not to be a victim? Couldn't I learn to be happy?

Slowly, I started to realize the role that I had been playing in my own life. I was the warden of my own prison and I could set myself free if I willed it. All I needed was the courage to believe in myself.

The courage that I needed was ultimately developed not in Niela's office but within the spiritual envelope of CODA, Co-Dependents Anonymous. CODA is a self-help 12-step program dealing with human relationships. It was Niela who suggested that I attend CODA meetings, and I consider that suggestion to be the second most important thing that she ever said to me. It led, ultimately, to the single greatest event of my transition.

I went to my first CODA meeting in November 1990, and almost walked back out. These people were talking about higher powers and spirituality--subjects I had no use for. I thought anybody who believed in God's mercy was a fool, and I would have none of it. I went back for more meetings, though, because it gave me a forum in which I could openly talk about my gender issues. Secretly, in one of the most inaccessible regions of my heart I wanted to believe in God's mercy. I wanted to believe that there was a greater power outside myself who could help me change, because I couldn't seem to change myself.

Each week I would attend CODA meetings and listen to other attendees tell how their relationship with a high power had changed their lives. Each week I would try and believe, hoping that my life would change also. Sometimes I actually would believe for brief periods, measured initially in hours, later in days.

I started to believe that I could change, and, once believing it, I actually did start to change.

In August 1992 I filed for divorce.

I started hormones in October 1993 and separated from my wife in November 1993.

In March of 1994 I "came out" at work, and in June I marched behind a "Transgendered and Proud" sign at the Boston Gay Pride parade.

Then, in late June, it happened. My higher power, my personal image of God, spoke to me. I didn't hear voices, there was no burning bush, but there was contact. My God showed me that my life had purpose and that I was not an accident.

I'm transgendered because I'm supposed to be transgendered--this is my place in the universe. My lifelong struggle to find myself, to find God, was over. I was now ready for the rest of my life.

On October 7, 1994, I started living full time as a woman.

STEPHANIE: Transsexual Woman Born Biological Male

I suppose the first thing I ought to say is that I started with therapy for the sole purpose of meeting the requirements of the Standards of Care. The SOC are pretty explicit about therapy. So what I was doing was meeting a prerequisite for hormones and later surgery--"punching a ticket," if you will. I would not have gone into therapy otherwise.

I had the same view of therapists that I do about surgeons: the only time one goes to see a surgeon is if one needs surgery. There is no commonly accepted idea about getting a mental health checkup, certainly not like getting a physical, having one's teeth cleaned, or changing the car's oil. I didn't feel as though I was mentally ill, and who goes to see a therapist (or a shrink) unless one is sick? That is the common perception, right?

OK, so I was wrong. She, in effect, held a mirror up to me, one in which I could see my soul. I was scared of that going in. I felt I had some pretty dark corners of my personality that would not be nice to contemplate, the mental equivalent of "the dark side of the Force." That fear at least was wrong.

So where did therapy help? First off, it helped me be sure that I am indeed a transsexual. Nothing crystallizes feelings and emotions like having to express them. What's nebulous has to be made tangible to be expressed. Sometimes that was very hard.

There were times I left feeling completely drained, and I drove home mainly on autopilot. I had a lot of fears about this whole process, fears that, once verbally expressed, began to be

151

conquered. And, as I learned, nothing was as fearsome in execution as it was in anticipation.

I certainly needed help working up to telling my parents. I don't know if I would have told them when I did without therapy. It would have been far more awkward if I had waited and told them now, when I have breasts and very little facial hair, than it was telling them when I did, and that was hard enough. There was a lot of work about how I deal with my parents and how I've dealt with them in the past. That's probably off the topic, but it was very useful. Old patterns die hard, but at least I understand, or think I do, what's going on.

I also needed help in other areas. I was carrying around a lot of deeply submerged anger over my divorce several years ago. When we got into that, really got into it, it was very cathartic. It was a lot like sticking a needle into a dragon of anger and finding that it was really a soap bubble. Pop! It was gone. All those years I had been carrying those feelings around. It felt good to get rid of them. "What hump?" was the attitude I had; I didn't know I was still angry. I sure as hell was, though.

So why do I continue with therapy after two years? I've certainly lived up to the spirit and the letter of the SOC. I continue because it is very helpful to me to talk to someone who is a professional, a person who is as objective an observer as I can find. You know how hard that is to find, even these days? I've a new friend who sought me out on the Internet because I'm a TS; she needed to talk to someone about her boyfriend (he's TS). She wanted to talk to someone who didn't have to be taught what a TS is, let alone someone who wouldn't freak out.

Freak. Yes, to many we are. Have you ever heard a promo like this: "Transsexual Construction Workers," on the next _Donahue_?" There are a lot of us out there, I think, and many buy into the "freak and pervert" view much of society seems to have. We need people who won't freak out--therapists, social workers, counselors, psychiatrists, clergy. People who don't know anything about transsexuals and tranvestites beyond what's in DSM4 are no help. How many of us would need help if we weren't considered to be freaks? Probably not all that many.

I continue with therapy. I have a therapist who is objective but also cares about me. I trust her in a way that I can't trust anyone else to tell me when I'm fooling myself or not seeing reality. I trust that all she cares about is whether or not I am making informed choices that will keep me mentally healthy. I trust that if I had concluded that I wasn't a TS and would be happy living as a man, she'd help there, too.

Care about us. Know about us. Don't grind any axes on us. Don't pigeonhole us. We are people. We laugh, cry, love, hate, heal, and bleed just like you do. Some of us are nice people, some aren't.

We're just like you, after all.

[Stephanie has successfully completed SRS and has begun to prepare for a new career as an attorney.]

PART V

FUTURE TRENDS

"There's no use trying" she said: "one can't believe impossible things." "I daresay you haven't had much practice," said the Queen. "When I was your age, I always did it for half-an-hour a day. Why, sometimes I've believed as many as six impossible things before breakfast!"

Lewis Carroll...

The minority of any group or society is the growing edge of that society, its conscience, and its spiritual teacher.

Imagine a world where gender change and expression were free of shame or ridicule, just one of many diversities. How would this change the behavior or life of our clients and ourselves? Can we start living that way now?

This changed world will come about when enough people are willing to live as though society is the way they *imagine* it could be.

More people accept gayness as a legitimate lifestyle than they did 20 years ago, because enough gays decided to start living the lives they preferred, and to insist on their right to do so, in this "sweet land of liberty."

Counselors, look at your own stereotypes about different kinds of gender assignments--about women, about men, about sexuality. How do your own stereotypes affect your behavior?

Here are some of the questions posed by Kate Bornstein in her book, *Gender Outlaw* (See Appendix)

- Is the determination of one another's gender a "social responsibility?"

- Do we have the legal or moral right to decide and assign our own genders? Or does that right belong to the state, the church, and the medical profession?

- What does a man feel like? What does a woman feel like?

- What's your gender? When did you decide that?

- Have you ever thought what it might be like to be neither for a day? An hour? One minute?

- Is there anything about your gender or gender role that you don't like, or that gets in your way?

- Are there one or two qualities about another gender that are appealing to you, enough so that you'd like to incorporate those qualities into your daily life?

- What would happen to your life if you did that? How do you think people would respond to you? What would you feel if they did that?

- What does a person of another gender have that you can't have?

- Do you think a transgendered person is a former man or woman? Do you think they are still the gender they were?

A lot of books have been written recently about male and female communication. Debra Tannen's book *You Just Don't Understand* is a good example. And yet, all of us know of exceptions to those examples of what men and women usually do in a conversation. Sometimes it's exactly the opposite. Often conversational style is dictated more by personality than by gender, or whether a person is an introvert or an extrovert, or whether he or she is technically oriented or artistically oriented.

To make sense of our world, we do need to be able to be able to discern, to say "this thing is different from that," and "two of those things have certain points in common and are different in other ways." We also need to be able to see all our similarities despite the differences.

In my opinion, all violent behavior is based on categorical thinking which is the basis on which wars are fought and killing is justified. It requires a "we" and a "they."

Yet we need categories to make order out of chaos. We need post-modern philosophers and linguists to develop enough inclusive language and enough differentiating language so that we can understand each other and still operate in a world that is simultaneously local and nonlocal, specific and nonspecific.

In discussing gender, we say that a person can be both a man and a woman, can be some place in between, can be shifting from one to the other, can be neither, can be something else. A colleague of mine, Maureen O'Hara, has identified forty-seven (so far!) different genders or modes of gender expression!

What's happening with infertility clinics now implies that we're not even going to be able to say for too much longer that the women have babies of men who impregnate them through intercourse, or that what makes a woman a woman is the ability to bear children, or that she has to have the eggs in her body, or even that men and women have to be available to each other biologically as totally differentiated genders in order for the species to continue.

We're making babies in petri dishes now. All kinds of things are happening in the late 90's that were not recognizable fifty years ago. In the future it will seem archaic to us that there was only one way to reproduce, even though we may need the basic material (and the old-fashioned way may still be the most fun!).

I know about a couple who are transsexual both ways. John used to be "the woman" and Judy used to be "the man." When they decided they wanted a baby they were not far along in their hormone treatment, had not yet had sex reassignment surgery. They decided to stop taking hormones so that John could be impregnated by Judy. After having the child, they would continue their transitions and switch the "father" and "mother" roles. To even try to wrap your mind around something like this is so radical that most people are extremely far from being able to conceive of it.

Yet, this is our challenge in a post-modern society--to live with infinite diversity, with rapid changes, with the mystical alongside the scientific, the poetic with the prosaic.

For our gender clients, it means being able to envision and help create a world where one's full humanity is embraced and creative possibilities are infinite.

APPENDIX

- Helping Organizations: Gender Related

- Association for Humanistic Psychology

- Bibliography: Gender Related

- Bibliography: Humanistic and Jungian Psychology, Dream Work

- Benjamin Standards of Care

161

HELPING ORGANIZATIONS: Gender Related

AMERICAN EDUCATIONAL GENDER INFORMATION SERVICE, INC. (AEGIS)

P. O. Box 33724
Decatur, GA 30033-0724

Dallas Denny, Executive Director

Telephone: 770 939-2128 Business
               770 939-0244 Information & referrals
FAX: 770 939-1770

E-Mail: aegis@mindspring.com

To be on our electronic distribution list, send E-Mail to majordomo@lists.mindspring.com.

On the first line of the body of your message, include the following:
subscribe aegis-list (your E-Mail address)

Visit the AEGIS FTP Site:
Host: ftp.mindspring,com
User ID: anonymous
Password: (your E-Mail address)
Directory: /users/aegis

AEGIS, the successor of Erickson Educational Foundation, continues a 30-year tradition of providing quality information about transgender and transsexual issues. Founded in 1990 and located in Atlanta, GA, USA, AEGIS has 501 (c) (3) tax-exempt status. AEGIS houses the National (USA) Transgender Library &

Archive, maintains a 6,000+ item annotated bibliography on transgender/transsexualism, operates a telephone help line and electronic services on the internet, conducts research on transsexual and transgender issues, and serves as an advocate for its members and other transgender and transsexual persons. Membership in AEGIS IS $36 per year ($46 outside the U.S and Canada), and includes the excellent *Chrysalis: The Journal of Transgressive Gender Identities,* a quarterly newsletter, and other benefits.

AEGIS' bibliography was published in hardcover in 1994 by Garland Publishers with the title *Gender Dysphoria: A Guide to Research* (ISBN 08 153-0840-X).

In early 1996, AEGIS'newly formed publishing arm, Sullivan Press (named after late FTM activist Lou Sullivan), will publish *Recommended Guidelines for Transgender Care* by Gianna E. Israel and Donald Tarver II., M.D. The recommended Guidelines are the first comprehensive guidebook for the medical and psychological care of transgendered and transsexual persons.

INTERNATIONAL FOUNDATION FOR GENDER EDUCATION (IFGE)
P.O. Box 229
Waltham, MA 02154-0229

Telephone: 617 894-8340 or 617 899-2212

FAX: 617 899-5703
E-Mail   IFGE@world.std.com

The IFGE was founded in 1978 as an educational and charitable organization addressing crossdressing and transgender issues.

IFGE'S mission is to be a leading advocate and educational organization for promoting self-definition and free expression of individual gender identity, and changing the paradigm of gender identity by recognizing the distinction between sexual orientation and gender.

The most widely distributed magazine on transgender issues, *Transgender Tapestry Journal*, is published by IFGE. The publication provides a forum for reasoned discourse on gender and related social issues. For many people it provides initial contact with the transgender community.

The organization provides representation and education to professional service providers and organizations such as the American Psychiatric Association, the American Association of Sex Educators Counselors and Therapists, and the National Association of Social Workers. IFGE provides outreach and referrals for individuals seeking help, and provides financial support for projects such as the International Conference on Transgender Law and Employment Policy. IFGE also sponsors an annual "Coming Together-Working Together" convention.

AMERICAN ASSOCIATION OF SEX EDUCATORS, COUNSELORS, AND THERAPISTS (AASECT)
David G. Lister, Executive Director
435 Michigan Avenue, Suite 1717
Chicago, IL 60611

Telephone: 312 644-0828

Professionals concerned with sex education, counseling and therapy, students.

Seeks to develop competency and standards for sex educators, sex counselors, and sex therapists through training, education, and research.

HARRY BENJAMIN INTERNATIONAL GENDER DYSPHORIA ASSOCIATION, INC. (HBIGDA)
Alice Webb, MSW, Director
P. O. Box 1718
Sonoma, CA 95476

Telephone: 707 938-2871
Fax: 707 938-2871

Membership organization for professionals who work with persons with gender dysphoria. Those with gender dysphoria should contact AEGIS and/or IFGE (see this listing).

OUTREACH INSTITUTE OF GENDER STUDIES
Ari Kane, Director
126 Western Avenue
Suite 246
Augusta, ME 04330

Telephone: 207 621-0858

Publisher, outreach and education activities. Sponsors Fantasia Fair, an annual conference.
Note: Includes GAIN, a network for helping professionals

RENAISSANCE EDUCATION ASSOCIATION, INC.
987 Old Eagle School Road
Suite 719
Wayne, PA 19087

Telephone: 610 975-9119

Open transgender support group

SAN FRANCISCO GENDER INFORMATION
Christine Beatty
P.O. Box 423602
San Francisco, CA 94142

Telephone: 415 346-8157

Referrals

SEX INFORMATION AND EDUCATION COUNCIL OF THE U.S.
(SIECUS)
Debra Haffner, Executive Director
32 Washington Place
New York, NY 10003

Telephone: 212 673-3850

Objective is to promote and affirm the concept of human sexuality.

**SOCIETY FOR THE SCIENTIFIC STUDY OF SEX
(Quad-Ess)**
Howard J. Ruppel, Jr., Executive Director
P.O. Box 208
Mt. Vernon, IA 52314

Telephone: 319 895-8407

Professional organization for sexologists

**SOCIETY FOR THE SECOND SELF
(TRI-ESS)**
P.O. Box 194
Tulare, CA 93275

Telephone: 209 688-9246 (help line, Pacific Time Zone)
                   210 438-7788 (help line, Central Time Zone)

Organization for heterosexual crossdressers and partners
Note: Publication is <u>Femme Mirror</u>

**SOUTH-CENTRAL TRANSGENDER ALLIANCE REGION
(STAR) CONNECTION**
c/o Boulton & Park Society
P. O. Box 17
Bulverde, TX 78163

Telephone: 512 545-3668 (help line)

STAR is a coalition of support groups in Texas, Louisiana,
Oklahoma, and New Mexico.

SPOUSES, PARTNERS, INTERNATIONAL CONFERENCE FOR EDUCATION (S.P.I.C.E.)
Dr. Peggy Rudd
P.O. Box 5304
Katy, Texas

Telephone: 909 875-2687

Annual conference for wives and partners of crossdressers

HUMANISTIC PSYCHOLOGY

Humanistic psychology* focuses on the potential of the individual. It addresses the future, rather than the pathology or dysfunctions of the past.

This approach takes into account the whole person. Symptoms are considered secondary to health, spirituality, and creativity.

There are differences in the way humanistic couselors work. Some are process-oriented. They work with what's unfolding at the moment. Others are goal-oriented and operate more like coaches.

Another important distinction is that humanistic psychology is an educational rather than a medical model. Both counselors and clients learn from the situation. The most important thing is not technique, but a quality of presence, being fully there. This enhances learning and insight. Humanistic counselors believe the value of psychotherapy goes beyond helping neurotic and psychotic populations. It is relevant to healthy persons in exploring their human potential.

*My acknowledgment to Art Warmoth, past President of AHP, and other AHP colleagues who contributed some of these ideas.

The Association for Humanistic Psychology,* a 30-year-old organization, represents the Third Force in psychology. (The First Force was behaviorism, the Second Force was psychoanalysis.)

It advocates a whole person, multidimensional perspective that emphasizes the power of personal choice and encourages approaches that seek to further understand the richness and depth of the human experience, including the symbolic dimension of consciousness. Meaning, value, culture, personal decision, and responsibility are all valued. (Anyone, not just psychologists, who shares this value base can join and attend conferences.)

Humanistic psychology challenges the assumption that only what can be directly perceived and publicly measured has value. It implies a commitment to the use of research approaches that provide access to all characteristics of human existence. It focuses on human potential.

Representative proponents, therapists and/or practitioners include Abraham Maslow, Carl Rogers, Rollo May, Fritz Perls, Virginia Satir, and many others.

*AHP, 45 Franklin Street #315, San Francisco, CA 94102 Phone: 415 864-8850

BIBLIOGRAPHY - Gender Related

This is a basic list--there are many more books available through IFGE, The Outreach Institute, or Different Path Press

Allen, Mariette Pathy
TRANSFORMATIONS:
Crossdressers and Those Who Love Them
Dutton 1989

Bolin, Anne
IN SEARCH OF EVE
Transsexual Rites of Passage
Bergin and Garvey Publishers 1988

Bolin, Anne
TRANSCENDING AND TRANSGENDERING:
Male to Female Transsexuals, Dichotomy, and Diversity
Zone Books, distributed by MIT Press 1994

Bornstein, Kate
GENDER OUTLAW:
On Men, Women and the Rest of Us
Routledge 1994

Bullough, Vern L. and Bonnie Bullough
CROSSDRESSING, SEX AND GENDER
University of Pennsylvania Press 1993

Docter, Dr. Richard F.
TRANSVESTITES and TRANSSEXUALS
Toward a Theory of Cross-Gender Behavior
Plenum Press 1988

Fast, Irene
GENDER IDENTITY
The Analytic Press 1984   .

Feinberg, Leslie
TRANSGENDER LIBERATION:
A Movement Whose Time Has Come
New York: World View Forum

Garber, Marjorie, Ed.D
VESTED INTERESTS:
Crossdressing and Cultural Anxiety
Routledge 1992

Herdt, Gilbert (Ed)
THIRD SEX, THIRD GENDER:
Beyond Sexual Dimorphism in Culture and History
Zone Books, distributed by MIT Press

McClain, Jerry/Jeri
TO BE A WOMAN
Different Path Press, Boston 1992

Prince, Virginia
UNDERSTANDING CROSSDRESSING
Chevalier Publications, Los Angeles 1976

Roberts, Jo Ann
COPING WITH CROSSDRESSING:
Tools and Strategies for Partners in Committed Relationships
Creative Design Services, King of Prussia, PA 1992

Rudd, Peggy
CROSSDRESSING WITH DIGNITY:
The Case For Transcending Gender lines
PM Publishers, 1990

Rudd, Peggy
MY HUSBAND WEARS MY CLOTHES
PM Publishers, 1989

Stevens, Jennifer Anne
FROM MASCULINE TO FEMININE
AND ALL POINTS IN BETWEEN
Different Path Press, Boston 1990

Tannen, Debra
YOU JUST DON'T UNDERSTAND
Morrow 1990

Eakins, Barbara Westbrook
SEX DIFFERENCES IN HUMAN COMMUNICATIONS
Mifflin, 1978

TRANSGENDER TAPESTRY
Quarterly magazine published by IFGE
(See Helping Organizations)

BIBLIOGRAPHY

HUMANISTIC AND JUNGIAN PSYCHOLOGY

AHP PERSPECTIVES
Newsletter of the **Association for Humanistic Psychology**
San Francisco   Telephone: 415 864-8850

JOURNAL OF HUMANISTIC PSYCHOLOGY
Contact AHP

de Carvalho, R.
THE FOUNDERS OF HUMANISTIC PSYCHOLOGY
Praeger 1991

Johnson, Robert
INNER WORK
Harper and Row 1986

McNiff, Shaun
ART AS MEDICINE
Shambhala 1992

Mindell, Arnold
WORKING WITH THE DREAMING BODY
Routledge 1985

Perls, Frederick S. MD, PhD
GESTALT THERAPY VERBATIM
Real People Press 1969

Rhyne, Janie
THE GESTALT ART EXPERIENCE
Wadsworth 1973

Royce, J.R. and L.P. Mos (Eds.)
HUMANISTIC PSYCHOLOGY: CONCEPTS AND CRITICISMS
Plenum 1981

Severin (Ed.)
HUMANISTIC VIEWPOINTS IN PSYCHOLOGY
McGraw-Hill 1965

Sutich, A. and M. Vich (Eds.)
READINGS IN HUMANISTIC PSYCHOLOGY
Free Press 1969

Welch, I.D., G.A. Tate and F. Richards (Eds.)
HUMANISTIC PSYCHOLOGY: A SOURCE BOOK
Prometheus Books 1978

A Guide to the
Harry Benjamin International Gender Dysphoria
Association, Inc.'s
Standards of Care

In 1979, a concerned group of psychologists, physicians, and other caregivers met to formulate guidelines for the hormonal and surgical treatment of persons with gender dysphoria. The resulting Standards of Care have been regularly modified, most recently in 1990.

The standards provide a description of the basic steps a transgendered person should follow in seeking hormonal and surgical treatment.

Steps should be taken sequentially. There is no requirement to proceed further. It is entirely possible, for instance, to live as a member of the other sex without desiring or having genital modification surgery. Only if you desire additional medical procedures should you proceed to higher steps.

1. Diagnosis

Your first step is to see a licensed clinical behavioral scientist (psychologist, counselor, psychiatrist, or clinical social worker) with proven competence in the field. Evaluation must occur over a period of at least ninety days. During this period, you should talk about your feelings of gender dysphoria with your therapist and explore your options.

After this ninety day period, you should ask your therapist for his diagnostic impressions.

2. Obtain referral for hormonal therapy

At the end of the ninety day period, you can also ask your therapist for a referral to an endocrinologist for hormonal therapy. An experienced therapist will have a referral network of endocrinologists and other professionals. Typically, the therapist will contact the endocrinologist on your behalf.

It will be a good idea to maintain contact with your therapist. First, sex reassignment is at best a difficult process, and there may be times when it will be useful to speak to a therapist. Second, there may be times when additional authorization letters or referrals are needed. In either case, a therapist who is familiar with your progress will be better able to help.

3a. Consult an endocrinologist

Your endocrinologist should have proven competence in working with transgendered persons, for improper dosages of hormones can be dangerous. Hormones will cause gradual but progressive changes in your secondary sex characteristics (breast growth and lessening of body hair in genetic males, and lowering of voice, and increase in body and facial hair in genetic females), which will cause you to look more masculine or feminine over time. Males will additionally experience lowered libido and sterility, and females will experience clitoral growth, increased libido, cessation of menses, and (sometimes) acne or male pattern baldness..

In males, hormonal changes, with the exception of breast growth, are largely reversible. Beard growth, voice deepening, and clitoral enlargement in females are not reversible.

Hormones for males consist of estrogens, and sometimes progestins. Anti-androgens may also be given. Route of administration may be oral, intramuscular, via injection, or transdermal, via patches. Androgens are given for females, usually intramuscularly.

All hormonal treatments require medical supervision.

3b. Start electrolysis (for males)

Males will need electrolysis to remove facial hair. This procedure is more easily done while still living in the male role, as it requires a two-four day period of growth before treatment, and can result in skin inflammation. When living as a female, it is difficult to schedule enough time to allow facial hair to grow for treatment.

Body hair will decrease with time on hormones, but some electrolysis of the arms, legs, or torso may be desired.

4 Begin a period of crossliving.

A major requirement of the Standards of Care is to live and work (or go to school, if a student) full time in the new gender role in order to achieve candidacy for genital surgery. During this "real-life test" you must dress and function in your new role 24 hours a day.

With sufficient time on hormones and (for males) electrolysis, appearance will change sufficiently to allow you to begin the real-life test. You should think of the real-life test as an experiment. It is not an endurance contest, but an opportunity to experience what life is like in the new gender. The more thoroughly you experience this new life, the better your idea of what the rest of your life will be like. If you find it necessary to revert to your original role on occasion, if you experience public humiliation because of your appearance, or if you find the new role nerve wracking or uncomfortable, this is a sign that you should extend the period of real-life test. Only when you are comfortable in the role and have been so for a minimum of one year should you consider scheduling genital modification surgery.

5. Sex Reassignment Surgery.

After the requirements of the real-life test have been met, you are eligible for evaluation for sex reassignment surgery.

Two authorization letters from therapists are required for sex reassignment surgery. Surgeons may have additional requirements.

For males, surgery can consist of a simple castration, but more frequently, a neovagina is constructed from penile and scrotal tissue. Penile inversion surgery is the most common vaginoplasty technique. Some surgeons supplement penile inversion with a skin graft or skin flap, and others with a section of large or small intestine.

For females, "top" surgery consists of breast reduction. There are several options for "bottom" surgery. Genitoplasty (metadioiplasty) converts the testosterone-enlarged clitoris into a small phallus. In phalloplasty, tissue from other areas of the body are used to create a phallus. Labia may be fused to form a scrotum, with silicon testicular implants.

Other Procedures

Males may desire additional plastic surgical procedures, such as breast implants, rhinoplasty (nose reduction), tracheal shave, hair flap surgery, or **facial or** body recontouring. Females may seek electrolysis on areas of the body which will be used as donor sites for phalloplasty. These procedures may be obtained at any time after the initiation of hormonal therapy. It is a good idea, however, to delay breast augmentation for at least two years after initiation of hormonal therapy, to allow for natural breast development.

Costs

Costs of medical treatment vary greatly. Many insurance companies specifically exclude many of the treatments associated with sex reassignment surgery. Typically the individual must bear many costs himself or herself. Indirect costs (loss of employment, legal costs like alimony and child support, etc.) can run far more than direct costs. By comparison shopping and in general being a good medical consumer, you can minimize direct costs. Careful planning can minimize indirect costs.

Support

Friends, family, sexual partners, and co- workers may or may not be supportive—but are sure to need information and support as well. Sources for support include helping professionals, support groups, and information services like AEGIS. You should avail yourself of as many as possible.

1995 by American Educational Gender Information Service, Inc.
AEGIS
P.O. Box33724
(770) 939-2128 Business(770)939-0244Information & Referrals
(770) 939-3357FAX
aegis@mindspringcom e-mail

186

Standards of Care: The Hormonal and Surgical Sex Reassignment of Gender Dysphoric Persons

1. Introduction

As of the beginning of 1979, an undocumentable estimate of the number of adult Americans hormonally and surgically sex-reassigned ranged from 3,000 to 6,000. Also undocumentable is the estimate that between 30,000 and 60,000 U.S.A. citizens consider themselves to be valid candidates for sex reassignment. World estimates are not available. As of mid-1978, approximately 40 centers in the Western hemisphere offered surgical sex reassignment to persons having a multiplicity of behavioral diagnoses applied under a multiplicity of criteria.

In recent decades, the demand for sex reassignment has increased as have the number and variety of possible psychologic, hormonal and surgical treatments. The rationale upon which such treatments are offered have become more and more complex. Varied philosophies of appropriate care has been suggested by various professionals identified as experts on the topic of gender identity. However, until the present, no statement of the standard of care to be offered to gender dysphoric patients (sex reassignment applicants) has received official sanction by any identifiable professional group. The present document is designed to fill that void.

2. Statement of Purpose

Harry Benjamin International Gender Dysphoria Association, Inc., presents the following as its explicit statement on the appropriate standards of care to be offered to applicants for hormonal and surgical sex reassignment.

3. Definitions

3.1 Standard of care. The standards of care, as listed below, are *minimal* requirements and are not to be construed as optimal standards of care. It is recommended that professionals involved in the management of sex reassignment cases use the following as *minimal* criteria for the evaluation of their work. It should be noted that some experts on gender identity recommend that the time parameters listed below should be

187

doubled, or tripled. It is recommended that the reasons for any exceptions to these standards, in the management of any individual case, be very carefully documented. Professional opinions differ regarding the permissibility of, and the circumstances warranting, any such exception

3.2 *Hormonal sex reassignment.* Hormonal sex reassignment refers to the administration of androgens to genotypic and phenotypic females, and the administration of estrogens and/or progesterones to genotypic and phenotypic males, for the purpose of effecting somatic changes in order for the patient to more closely approximate the physical appearance of the genotypically other sex. Hormonal sex-reassignment does not refer to the administration of hormones for the purpose of medical care andlor research conducted for the treatment or study of non-gender dysphoric medical conditions (e.g., aplastic anemia, impotence, cancer, etc.).

3.3 *Surgical sex reassignment.* Genital surgical sex reassignment refers to surgery of the genitalia and/or breasts performed for the purpose of altering the morphology in order to approximate the physical appearance of the genetically-other sex in persons diagnosed as gender dysphoric. Such surgical procedures as mastectomy, reduction mammoplasty, augmentation mammoplasty, castration, orchidectomy, penectomy, vaginoplasty, hysterectomy, salpingectomy, vaginectomy, oophorectomy and phalloplasty-in the absence of any diagnosable birth defect or other medically defined pathology, except gender dysphoria, are included in this category labeled surgical sex reassignment.

Non-genital surgical sex reassignment refers to any and all other surgical procedures of non-genital, or non-breast sites (nose, throat, chin, cheeks, hips, etc.) conducted for the purpose of effecting a more masculine appearance in a genetic female or for the purpose of effecting a more feminine appearance in a genetic male, in the absence of identifiable pathology which would warrant such surgery regardless of the patient's genetic sex (facial injuries, hermaphroditism, etc.).

3.4 *Gender Dysphoria.* Gender Dysphoria herein refers to that psychological state whereby a person demonstrates dissatisfaction with their sex of birth and the sex role, as socially defined, which applies to that sex, and who requests hormonal and surgical sex reassignment. Gender

188

dysphoria, herein, does not refer to cases of infant sex reassignment or reannouncement. Gender dysphoria, therefore, is the primary working diagnosis applied to any and all persons requesting surgical and hormonal sex reassignment.

3.5 Clinical behavioral scientist. * Possession of an academic degree in a behavioral science does not necessarily attest to the possession of sufficient training or competence to conduct psychotherapy, psychologic counseling, nor diagnosis of gender identity problems. Persons recommending sex reassignment surgery or hormone therapy should have documented training and experience in the diagnosis and treatment of a broad range of psychologic conditions. Licensure or certification as a psychological therapist or counselor does not necessarily attest to competence in sex therapy. Persons recommending sex reassignment surgery or hormone therapy should have the documented training and experience to diagnose and treat a broad range of sexual conditions. Certification in sex therapy or counseling does not necessarily attest to competence in the diagnosis and treatment of gender identity conditions or disorders. Persons recommending sex reassignment surgery or hormone therapy should have proven competence in general psychotherapy, sex therapy, and gender counseling/therapy.

Any and all recommendations for sex reassignment surgery and hormone therapy should be made only by clinical behavioral scientists possessing the following minimal documentable credentials and expertise:

3.5.1. A minimum of a Masters Degree in a clinical behavioral science, granted by an institution of education accredited by a national or regional accrediting board.

3.5.2. One recommendation, of the two required for sex reassignment surgery, must be made by a person possessing a doctoral degree (e.g., Ph.D.,

---

*The drafts of these Standards of Care dated 2/79 and 1/80 require that all recommendations for hormonal and/or surgical sex reassignment be made by licensed psychologists or psychiatrists. That requirement was rescinded, and replaced by the definition in section 3.5, in 3/81.

Ed.D., D.Sc., D.S.W., Psy.D., or M.D.) in a clinical behavioral science, granted by an institution of education accredited by a national or regional accrediting board.

3.5.3. Demonstrated competence in psychotherapy as indicated by a license to practice medicine, psychology, clinical social work, marriage and family counseling, or social psychotherapy, etc., granted by the state of residence. In states where no such appropriate license board exists, persons recommending sex reassignment surgery or hormone therapy should have been certified by a nationally known and reputable association, based on education and experience criteria, and, preferably, some form of testing (and not simply on membership received for dues paid) as an accredited or certified therapist/counselor (e.g. American Board of Psychiatry and Neurology, Diplomate in Psychology from the American Board of Professional Psychologists, Certified Clinical Social Workers, American Association of Marriage and Family Therapists, American Professional Guidance Association, Licensed Mental Health Counselors).

3.5.4. Demonstrated specialized competence in sex therapy and theory as indicated by documentable training and supervised clinical experience in sex therapy (in some states professional licensure requires training in human sexuality; also, persons should have approximately the training and experience as required for certification as a Sex Therapist or Sex Counselor by the American Association of Sex Educators, Counselors and Therapists, or as required for membership in the Society for Sex Therapy and Research). Continuing education in human sexuality and sex therapy should also be demonstrable.

3.5.5. Demonstrated and specialized competence in therapy, counseling, and diagnosis of gender identity disorders as documentable by training and supervised clinical experience, along with continuing education.

The behavioral scientists recommending sex reassignment surgery and hormone therapy and the physician and surgeon(s) who accept those recommendations share responsibility for certifying that the recommendations are made based on competency indicators as described above.

190

4. Principles and Standards

Introduction

4.1.1 **Principle 1.** Hormonal and surgical sex reassignment is extensive in its effects, is invasive to the integrity of the human body, has effects and consequences which are not, or are not readily, reversible, and may be requested by persons experiencing short-termed delusions or beliefs which may later be changed and reversed.

4.1.2. **Principle 2.** Hormonal and surgical sex reassignment are procedures requiring justification and are not of such minor consequence as to be performed on an elective basis.

4.1.3. **Principle** 3. Published and unpublished case histories are known in which the decision to undergo hormonal and surgical sex reassignment was, after the fact, regretted and the final result of such procedures proved to be psychologically dehabilitating to the patients.

4.1.4. **Standard 1.** Hormonal and/or surgical* sex reassignment on demand (i.e., justified simply because the patient has requested such procedures) is contraindicated. It is herein declared to be professionally improper to conduct, offer, administer or perform hormonal sex reassignment and/ or surgical sex reassignment without careful evaluation of the patient's reasons for requesting such services and evaluation of the beliefs and attitudes upon which such reasons are based.

4.2.1 **Principle 4.** The analysis or evaluation of reasons, motives, attitudes, purposes, etc., requires skills not usually associated with the professional training of persons other than clinical behavioral scientists.

---

*The present standards provide no guidelines for the granting of non-genital/breast cosmetic or reconstructive surgery. The decision to perform such surgery is left to the patient and surgeon. The original draft of this document did recommend the following however (rescinded 1/80): "Non-genital sex reassignment (facial, hip, limb, etc.) shall be preceded by a period of at least 6 months during which time the patient lives full-time in the social role of the genetically other sex."

4.2.2. **Principle 5.** Hormonal and/or surgical sex reassignment is performed for the purpose of improving the quality of life as subsequently experienced and such experiences are most properly studied and evaluated by the clinical behavioral scientist.

4.2.3. **Principle** 6. Hormonal and surgical sex reassignment are usually offered to persons, in part, because a psychiatric/psychologic diagnosis of transsexualism (see DSM-III, section 302.5X), or some related diagnosis, has been made. Such diagnoses are properly made only by clinical behavioral scientists.

4.2.4. **Principle** 7. Clinical behavioral scientists, in deciding to make the recommendation in favor of hormonal and/or surgical sex reassignment share the moral responsibility for that decision with the physician and/or surgeon who accepts that recommendation.

4.2.5. **Standard 2.** Hormonal and surgical (genital and breast) sex reassignment must be preceded by a firm written recommendation for such procedures made by a clinical behavioral scientist who can justify making such a recommendation by appeal to training or professional experience in dealing with sexual disorders, especially the disorders of gender identity and role.

4.3.1. **Principle** 8. The clinical behavioral scientist's recommendation for hormonal and/or surgical sex reassignment should, in part, be based upon an evaluation of how well the patient fits the diagnostic criteria for transsexualism as listed in the DSM-III-R category 302.50 to wit:

> "A. Persistent discomfort and sense of inappropriateness about one's assigned sex.
>
> B. Persistent preoccupation for at least two years with getting rid of one's primary and secondary sex characteristics and acquiring the sex characteristics of the other sex.
>
> C. The person has reached puberty."

This definition of transsexualism is herein interpreted not to exclude persons who meet the above criteria but who otherwise may, on the basis of their past behavioral histories, be conceptualized and classified as transvestites and/or effeminate male homosexuals or masculine female homosexuals.

4.3.2. **Principle 9.** The intersexed patient (with a documented hormonal or genetic abnormality) should first be treated by procedures commonly accepted as appropriate for such medical conditions.

4.3.3. **Principle 10.** The patient having a psychiatric diagnosis (i.e., schizophrenia) in addition to a diagnosis of transsexualism should first be treated by procedures commonly accepted as appropriate for such non-transsexual psychiatric diagnoses.

4.3.4. **Standard 3.** Hormonal and surgical sex reassignment may be made available to intersexed patients and to patients having non-transsexual psychiatric/psychologic diagnoses if the patient and therapist have fulfilled the requirements of the herein listed standards; if the patient can be reasonably expected to be habilitated or rehabilitated, in part, by such hormonal and surgical sex reassignment procedures; and if all other commonly accepted therapeutic approaches to such intersexed or non-transsexual psychiatrically/psychologically diagnosed patients have been either attempted, or considered for use prior to the decision not to use such alternative therapies. The diagnosis of schizophrenia, therefore, does not necessarily preclude surgical and hormonal sex reassignment.

Hormonal Sex Reassignment

4.4.1. **Principle 11.** Hormonal sex reassignment is both therapeutic and diagnostic in that the patient requesting such therapy either reports satisfaction or dissatisfaction regarding the results of such therapy.

4.4.2. **Principle 12.** Hormonal sex reassignment is both therapeutic and diagnostic in that the patient requesting such therapy either reports satisfaction or dissatisfaction regarding the results of such therapy.

4.4.3. **Principal 13.** Hormonal sex reassignment should precede surgical sex reassignment as its effects (patient satisfaction or dissatisfaction) may indicate or contraindicate later surgical sex reassignment.

4.4.4 **Standard 4.*** The initiation of hormonal sex reassignment shall be preceded by recommendation for such hormonal therapy, made by a clinical behavioral scientist.

4.5.1. **Principal 14.** The administration of androgens to females and of estrogens and/or progesterones to males may lead to mild or serious health-threatening complications.

4.5.2 **Principle 15.** Persons who are in poor physical health, or who have identifiable abnormalities in blood chemistry, may be at above average risk to develop complications should they receive hormonal medication.

4.5.3 **Standard 5.** The physician prescribing hormonal medication to a person for the purpose of effecting hormonal sex reassignment must warn the patient of possible negative complications which may arise and that physician should also make available to the patient (or refer the patient to a facility offering) monitoring of relevant blood chemistries and routine physical examinations including, but not limited to, the measurement of SGPT in persons receiving testosterone and the measurement of SGPT, bilirubin, triglycerides and fasting glucose in persons receiving estrogens.

4.6.1. **Principle 16.** The diagnostic evidence for transsexualism (see 4.3.1. above) requires that the clinical behavioral scientist have knowledge, independent of the patient's verbal claim, that the dysphoria, discomfort, sense of inappropriateness and wish to be rid of one's own genitals have existed for at least two years. This evidence may be obtained by interview of the patient's appointed informant (friend or relative) or it may best be obtained by the fact

---

*This standard, in the original draft, recommended that the patient must have lived successfully in the social/gender role of the genetically other sex for at least 3 months prior to the initiative of hormonal sex reassignment. This requirement was rescinded 1/80.

that the clinical behavioral scientist has professionally known the patient for an extended period of time.

4.6.2. **Standard 6**. The clinical behavioral scientist making the recommendation in favor of hormonal sex reassignment shall have known the patient in a psychotherapeutic relationship for at least 3 months prior to making said recommendation.

Surgical (Genital andlor Breast) Sex Reassignment

4.7.1. **Principle 17**. Peer review is a commonly accepted procedure in most branches of science and is used primarily to ensure maximal efficiency and correctness of scientific decisions and procedures.

4.7.2. **Principle 18**. Clinical behavioral scientists must often rely on possibly unreliable or invalid sources of information (patients' verbal reports or the verbal reports of the patients' families and friends) in making clinical decisions and in judging whether or not a patient has fulfilled the requirements of the herein listed standards.

4.7.3. **Principle 19**. Clinical behavioral scientists given the burden of deciding who to recommend for hormonal and surgical sex reassignment and for whom to refuse such recommendations are subject to extreme social pressure and possible manipulation as to create an atmosphere in which charges of laxity, favoritism, sexism, financial gain, etc., may be made.

4.7.4. **Principle 20**. A plethora of theories exist regarding the etiology of gender dysphoria and the purposes or goals of hormonal and/or surgical sex reassignment such that the clinical behavioral scientist making the decision to recommend such reassignment for a patient does not enjoy the comfort or security of knowing that his or her decision would be supported by the majority of his or her peers.

4.7.5. **Standard 7**. The clinical behavioral scientist recommending that a patient applicant receive surgical (genital and breast) sex reassignment must obtain peer review, in the format of a clinical behavioral scientist peer who will personally examine the patient applicant, on at least one occasion, and who will, in writing state

195

that he or she concurs with the decision of the original clinical behavioral scientist. Peer review (a second opinion) is not required for hormonal sex reassignment. Non-genital/breast surgical sex reassignment does not require the recommendations of a behavioral scientist. At least one of the two behavioral scientists making the favorable recommendation for surgical (genital and breast) sex reassignment must be a doctoral level clinical behavioral scientist*

4.9.1 **Standard 9.** Genital sex reassignment shall be preceded by a period of at least 12 months during which time the patient lives full time in the social role of the genetically other sex.

4.10.1. **Principle 21.** Genital surgical sex reassignment includes the invasion of, and the alteration of, the genitourinary tract. Undiagnosed pre-existing genitourinary disorders may complicate later genital surgical sex reassignment.

4.10.2. **Standard 10.*** Prior to genital surgical sex reassignment a urological examination should be conducted for the purpose of identifying and perhaps treating abnormalities of the genitourinary tract.

4.11.1 **Standard 11.** The physician administering or performing surgical (genital) sex reassignment is guilty of professional misconduct if he or she does not receive written recommendations in favor of such procedures from at least two clinical behavioral scientists; at least one of which is a doctoral level clinical behavioral scientist and one of whom has known the patient in a professional relationship for at least 6 months.

Miscellaneous

4.12.1. **Principle 22.** The care and treatment of sex reassignment applicants or patients often causes special problems for the professionals offering such care and treatment. These special problems include, but are not limited to, the need for the

---

* In the original and V80 version of these standards, one of the clinical behavioral scientists was required to be a psychiatrist. That requirement was rescinded in 3/81.
**This requirement was rescinded 1/90.

196

professional to cooperate with education of the public to justify his or her work, the need to document the case history perhaps more completely than is customary in general patient care, the need to respond to multiple, nonpaying, service applicants and the need to be receptive and responsive to the extra demands for services and assistance often made by sex reassignment applicants as compared to other patient groups.

4.12.2. **Principle 23.** Sex reassignment applicants often have need for post-therapy (psychologic, hormonal and surgical) follow-up care for which they are unable or unwilling to pay.

4.12.3. **Principle 24.** Sex reassignment applicants often are in a financial status which does not permit them to pay excessive professional fees.

4.12.4. **Standard 12.** It is unethical for professionals to charge sex reassignment applicants "whatever the traffic will bear" or excessive fees far beyond the normal fees charged for similar services by the professional. It is permissible to charge sex reassignment applicants for services in advance of the tendering of such services even if such an advance fee arrangement is not typical of the professional's practice. It is permissible to charge patients, in advance, for expected services such as post-therapy follow-up care and/or counseling. It is unethical to charge patients for services which are essentially research and which services do not directly benefit the patient.

4.13.1. **Principle 25.** Sex reassignment applicants often experience social, legal and financial discrimination not known, at present, to be prohibited by federal or state law.

4.13.2. **Principle 26.** Sex reassignment applicants often must conduct formal or semiformal legal proceedings (i.e., in-court appearances against insurance companies or in pursuit of having legal documents changed to reflect their new sexual and genderal status, etc.).

4.13.3. **Principle 27.** Sex reassignment applicants, in pursuit of what are assumed to be their civil rights as citizens, are often in need of assistance (in the form of copies of records, letters of endorsement, court testimony, etc.) from the professionals involved in their case.

4.13.4. **Standard 13.** It is permissible for a professional to charge only the normal fee for services needed by a patient in pursuit of his or her civil rights. Fees should not be charged for services for which, for other patient groups, such fees are not normally charged.

4.14.1. **Principle 28.** Hormonal and surgical sex reassignment has been demonstrated to be a rehabilitative, or habilitative, experience for properly selected adult patients.

4.14.2 **Principle 29.** Hormonal and surgical sex reassignment are procedures which must be requested by, and performed only with the agreement of, the patient having informed consent. Sex reannouncement or sex reassignment procedures conducted on infantile or early childhood intersexed patients are common medical practices and are not included in or affected by the present discussion.

4.14.3 **Principle 30.** Sex reassignment applicants often, in their pursuit of sex reassignment, believe that hormonal and surgical sex reassignment have fewer risks than such procedures are known to have.

4.14.4. **Standard 14.** Hormonal and surgical sex reassignment may be conducted or administered only to persons obtaining their legal majority (as defined by state law) or to persons declared by the courts as legal adults (emancipated minors).

4.15.1 **Standard 15.** Hormonal and surgical sex reassignment may be conducted or administered only after the patient applicant has received full and complete explanations, preferably in writing, in words understood by the patient applicant, of all risks inherent in the requested procedures.

4.16.1. **Principle 31.** Gender dysphoric sex reassignment applicants and patients enjoy the same rights to medical privacy as does any other patient group.

4.16.2. **Standard 16.** The privacy of the medical record of the sex reassignment patient shall be safeguarded according to procedures in use to safeguard the privacy of any other patient group.

5. Explication

5.1.   Prior to the initiation of hormonal sex reassignment.

5.1.1.   The patient must demonstrate that the sense of discomfort with the self and demonstrate that the sense of discomfort with the self and the urge to rid the self of the genitalia and the wish to live in the genetically other sex role have existed for at **least 2 years.**

5.1.2.   The patient must be known to a clinical behavioral scientist for at least 3 months and that clinical behavioral scientist must endorse the patient's request for hormone therapy

5.1.3   Prospective patients should receive a complete physical examination which includes, but is not limited to, the measurement of SGPT in persons to receive testosterone and the measurement of SGPT, bilirubin, triglycerides and fasting glucose in persons to receive estrogens.

5.2.   Prior to the initiation of genital or breast sex reassignment (Penectomy, orchidectomy, castration, vaginoplasty, mastectomy, hysterectomy, oophorectomy, salpingectomy, vaginectomy, phalloplasty, reduction mammoplasty, breast amputation):

5.2.1. See 5.1.1., above.

5.2.2. The patient must be known to a clinical behavioral scientist for at least 6 months and that clinical behavioral scientist must endorse the patient's request for genital surgical sex reassignment.

5.2.3. The patient must be evaluated at least once by a clinical behavioral scientist other than the clinical behavioral scientist specified in 5.2.2. above and that second clinical behavioral scientist must endorse the patient's request for genital sex reassignment. At least one of the clinical behavioral scientists making the recommendation for genital sex reassignment must be a doctoral level clinical behavioral scientist.

5.2.4. The patient must have been successfully living in the genetically other sex role for *at least* one year.

5.3. During and after services are provided:

5.3. The patient's right to privacy should be honored.

5.3.2. The patient must be charged only appropriate fees and these fees may be levied in advance of services.

IDSM-III-R Diagnostic and Statistical Manual of Mental Disorders (Third Edition-Revised) Washington, D.C. The American Psychiatric Association, 1987.

Original draft dated
February 13, 1979

Revised draft (1/90) dated
January 20, 1980

Revised draft (3/81)
dated March 9, 1981

Revised draft (1/90) dated
January 25, 1990